WAR IN THE FALKLANDS

The campaign in pictures

By The Sunday Express Magazine team

Weidenfeld and Nicolson · London

Cover pictures: Front: Men of 40 Commando raising the flag at Port Howard on West Falklands in the final act of Argentine surrender. *Back:* Rescuing survivors of Sir Galahad at Bluff Cove.

Front Endpaper: 2 Para setting off at dusk on their march from Sussex Mountain to Goose Green.

First published in 1982 in Great Britain by

George Weidenfeld and Nicolson Limited
91 Clapham High Street, London SW4 7TA

Copyright © The Sunday Express Ltd 1982

ISBN 0 297 78202 9

Designed by Tony Garrett and Ewing Paddock

Separations by Newsele Litho Ltd
Printed in Great Britain by Redwood Burn Ltd
Typeset and bound by Butler & Tanner Ltd, Frome and London

Contents

Introduction

For three months in the spring and summer of 1982, the Falklands conflict was headline news across the world. It was the first conventional war that British troops had fought since Korea. It was a war that saw great heroism, great sacrifice, great tragedy – and a lot of harsh lessons for the fighting services and their equipment.

Yet in some respects it was a mysterious war. Unlike the conflicts of Vietnam and the Middle East, observed in minutest detail by photographers of the international press, it was a war that received limited media coverage. Only two professional Fleet Street photographers and two television crews accompanied the Task Force. They produced some memorable images, but simply because they could not be in a dozen places at once their pictorial record is incomplete.

This book seeks to fill that gap. The reason it can do so is the democratisation of the camera. Many officers and men of the fighting services carried, metaphorically, a Nikon in their knapsacks. And it has become the custom for ships and combat units to be accompanied by their own photographers gathering material for training and record purposes. As they returned from the war, each major combat unit was contacted by researchers of The Sunday Express Magazine, and many thousands of their transparencies have been sifted and edited. The war as seen by the media has thus been augmented by the graphic record of the combatants themselves.

Paradoxically, because so many of these pictures were the result not of the disengaged skills of the professionals, but of the deeply involved eyes of soldiers, sailors, airmen and Marines photographing their comrades, they convey a truer and more affecting reflection of the nature of modern warfare. It is a kaleidoscope of war that may lack the heroics of a Robert Capa or the despair of a Donald McCullin, but which perhaps more accurately conveys the slog and the grind and the attention to logistic detail which are at the heart of any successful military campaign.

The men who contributed to this book also gave their accounts of the circumstances in which their pictures had been taken. Their stories, on which the captions and commentaries are largely based, confirm the view, disseminated at the time, of British fighting men of high skill and morale, superbly trained. But they also reveal that the outcome of the war was more of a 'damned close-run thing' than we realised or cared to contemplate. Their realism gives us a deeper appreciation of their heroism.

Ron Hall, Editor, Sunday Express Magazine

An unlikely battlefield

'But why do you want the Falklands?' a British minister once asked his Argentine counterpart. 'You know that scarcely anybody lives in the part of Argentina which is like them.' He was talking about Patagonia in the south of the country. 'Besides,' he went on, 'half of those people are Welsh.' He stabbed his finger at the Argentine. 'Would *you* live on the islands?' he asked. The exquisite Argentine recoiled. 'You do not understand,' he said stiffly. 'We are talking about a principle.'

The Falkland Islands are among the loveliest places on earth: two big and 200 tiny islands, half the size of Wales. A wildlife paradise 300 miles off the Argentine coast and 8,000 miles from Britain. The gateway to Antarctica. The capital, Stanley, is the southernmost city in the world: the cathedral is rather grand. For 150 years, Britons have lived there. A hard life. Plain farming people.

Yet the Falklands are in decline. Population has fallen steadily until now, at 1,800 – 1,300 born there – it is almost too small to be viable. Their staple exports are the wool and skins of sheep; yet the sheep decline too: there are half what the grazing would support. More than two-thirds of the world's protein needs and double its present white-fish catch could be harvested from their seas – the protein as tiny krill. There are no Falklands' trawlers. The islands' shores are besieged by kelp, a seaweed rich in minerals; yet a kelp-processing project collapsed. Tens of thousands of sheep carcasses are yearly dumped in the sea. Third World countries have asked about these. A mutton-processing plant lies abandoned.

Two factors explained much of this sad state. The first is that the Falklands are the last crofting community of the old kind. The Falkland Islands Company – its head office is in Britain – owns 43 per cent of the land; has a monopoly on all import and export shipments; a monopoly of shipping round the coasts too. Of the 28 non-Falkland Islands Company farms on the islands, the owners of only three lived there ten years ago; now the figure is 19 resident, so things are improving. Even so, only a few per cent of the islands' wealth, their gross national product, is put back into them.

And Argentina claims them with passion. That is the second factor in their decline. The dispute between Britain and Argentina has run for 150 years, but only in the last 20 years has Argentina's claim become a national crusade. Successive British Governments have never said 'yes' but never said 'no'. Their future uncertain, the Falklands and their people have languished – while Argentina grew impatient. Finally, a new Argentine president, General Leopoldo Galtieri, decided to take action. He ignored one thing. The Falklanders are British and wish to remain so.

'They are few in number, but they have the right to live in peace, to choose their own way of life and to determine their own allegiance.'

Mrs Thatcher, House of Commons, April 3, 1982

Scenes from Falklands life: the farm at Walker Creek, and the Globe Tavern, Stanley.

The atmosphere of Stanley: (*left to right*) the Philomel Store is down by the jetty; it will appear in later scenes, surrounded then by the debris of war; the Chief Secretary's house, with a lawn running down to one of the 300 wrecks which dot the Falklands coasts; the Operations Room at Moody Brook Barracks, west of Stanley, the base of the Royal Marine squad which was the islands' garrison. *Below:* the beach at Stanley in the tranquil times when the only invaders were duck.

The Argentine invasion

Colour Sergeant John Noone heard the shots as he paced the corridors of Government House. A Marine for 27 years – Malaya, Aden, Ulster – he effortlessly identified their type, their source and finally their significance. 'Christ,' he said, 'they've taken out the Brook.' He sprinted out the front door, down the gravel drive and over the cattle grid and stood in the road, listening. The night was mild, starlit. A light breeze blew, and in Stanley Bay the surf was breaking. Noone heard the other sounds – a thump of grenades, a long rattle of automatic fire – and he knew they signalled the Argentine invasion: 'I could hear a lot of men shouting. It was incoherent, but definitely a lot of men.' And he knew, by the direction of the noise, that the invaders had wrecked the Marines' plan for the defence of the Falklands' capital. The sounds were coming from the west – not from the east, as expected. The Argentines were shooting-up the Marines' own barracks at Moody Brook.

There was never any way in which the 61 men of Naval Party 8901, as the Marine detachment on the Falklands was obscurely called, could have won that night. Out in the Bay the Argentine aircraft carrier Veintecento de Mayo was just sailing in past the lighthouse. But they put up a good fight. They had been told in the evening that the invasion was coming. (That was why Noone and his comrades were alive and armed in Government House, rather than riddled in their beds in Moody Brook.) At his briefing their CO, Major Mike Norman, said to them: 'Remember, you're not fighting for the Falklands. This time, you're fighting for yourselves.' That was true. They fought for intangible reasons: pride; professionalism; obstinacy; the duty and

APRIL 2

'We have lots of new friends'

Falklands telex operator sending the news to London

Argentine Special Forces who made the first landing on the Falklands (*opposite*) told British Marines they captured that they had been training for the assault since February. It seems that Argentina's new ruler, General Galtieri, ordered planning for the landings while trying to discover through diplomatic talks whether Britain would ever give up the islands peacefully. He concluded they would not, so chose the military option. The battle was soon over (*left*). With help from an Argentine working in Stanley, Vice Comodoro Hector Gilobert, who ran the local airline office, a truce and then a surrender was arranged.

The Argentine invasion: Major Mike Norman's own map shows (*right*) how Argentine Special Forces wrecked his plan. He thought they would land at the beaches (1) by the airport. But they came into Mullet Creek (2) and, having destroyed the Marine barracks at Moody Brook (3), attacked Government House from the west. Only then did landing craft (4) come ashore by the airfield. Norman had posted his men (5) to conduct a fighting retreat down the airport road. The horseshoes are his symbols for defensive positions and the numbers by them are those of the Marine section holding each.

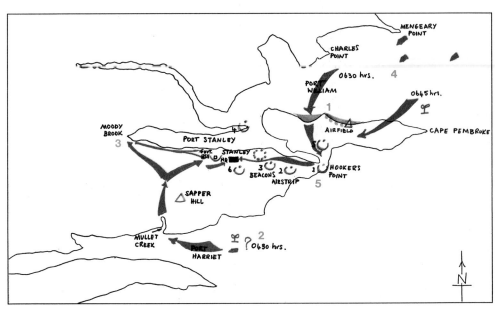

honour of a Royal Marine, mostly. And when, just after breakfast, they were ordered by a regretful Governor Rex Hunt to surrender, they felt oddly resentful. 'We thought "Christ, it's daylight. Now we could have them all",' said Noone.

Not even Noone really believed that. When 140 Argentine special forces landed about 4.30 am on Friday, April 2 at Mullet Creek, south-west of Stanley, made their stealthy way to the clump of huts at Moody Brook and blew them apart, Norman's tiny forces were mostly crouched in positions on the other side of town, along the road in from the airport. When the

On Governor Hunt's orders the Marines at Government House surrendered (*far left*) and were searched by the Argentines. The invasion commander, Admiral Carlos Busser, is on the right. Hunt refused to shake his hand, on the grounds that invasion was an ungentlemanly act. Busser had in his force an aircraft carrier and four destroyers so there could be only one outcome: Argentina's flag was raised over the Falklands (*left*).

Argentines landed on the beaches by the airport *after* the blowing of Moody Brook, Norman's men were pinned between troops coming both ways.

Hurriedly, the Marines scrambled back to Government House, to set about defending a white clapboard vicarage with a conservatory along its front and lawns bordered by a low stone wall. 'When I took up my fire position my mouth went a bit dry,' Noone recalled. 'The old tongue was rasping, the burning sensation and what have you. I got into a comfortable position, flicked up my sights and just sat there.' For 90 minutes, Argentine troops on a wooded knoll behind the house poured fire on them, but the

Marines in the house and behind the stone wall staved them off. Then about 7.30 am Noone heard a low rumble – and he knew what it was. The Argentines had landed light tanks: in fact, armoured personnel carriers armed with 30 mm cannon which could reduce Government House to rubble. 'We could have held them off if it hadn't been for the tanks,' Noone said wistfully. 'They could have had up to 600 guys out there and we could have brought them down like flies . . .'

It was all over. At 9.25 am, his residence surrounded by these vehicles, Hunt surrendered. The British troops were rounded up, searched and sent home via Montevideo.

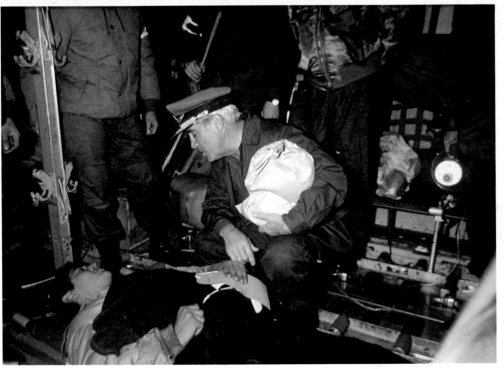

```
LDN    HELLO THERE WHAT ARE ALL THESE ROUMOURS WE HEAR  THIS IS LDN
                                                        - 2 APR 1982
FK      WE HAVE LOTS OF NEW FRIENDS
LDN    WHAT ABOUT INVASION RUMOURS
FK     THOSE ARE THE FRIENDS I WAS MEANING
LDN     THEY HAVE LANDED ?
FK     ABSOLUTELY
LDN     ARE YOU OPEN FOR TRAFFIC IE NORMAL TELEX SERVICE
FK     NO ORDERS ON THAT YET ONE MUST OBEY ORDERS
LDN    WHOSE ORDERS
FK     THE NEW GOVERNORS
LDN    ARGENTINA ?
FK     YES
LDN    ARE THE ARGENTINIANS IN CONTROL
FK     YES YOU CANT ARGUE WITH THOUSANDS OF TROOPS PLUS ENORMOUS
       NAVY SUPPORT WHEN YOU ARE ONLY 1800 STRONG
       STAND BY PSE
```

As the Marines sat under guard in the Government House paddock (*top left*), a telex operator at the local Cable & Wireless office tried desperately to send a veiled message to London about the invasion (*top right*). The Argentine troops rejoiced (*above*) and Admiral Busser went for a triumphal tour of Stanley (*centre*). It did not occur to them that the British would fight back. The Argentine casualties were flown home to the mainland (*far left*). Norman's Marines killed two of the invaders, wounded at least a dozen and, remarkably, destroyed an Argentine armoured vehicle during the retreat from the airport. 'We'll be back,' Governor Hunt promised.

The Argentine forces seemed unprepared for the harsh conditions on the islands. The Falklands winter was approaching, yet (*top left*) the troops had to live in flimsy tents. More troops flew in daily (*bottom left*) as reinforcements against a British assault. They could not really believe it would come, but they did believe Britain might launch naval bombardments, so their guns were massed along Stanley's seashore (*centre top*). The Argentines truly saw themselves as liberators of the islands and expected their inhabitants to welcome them (*top right*). Back on the mainland, it was hailed as a triumph, and patriotic mothers sent whole armies of cakes and comforts to the brave boys at last on the Malvinas (*left*).

Fall of South Georgia

When the Royal Navy's ice-patrol ship Endurance set out from Stanley early on Monday March 22, bound for a desolate whaling station 800 miles away in the icy splendour of South Georgia, nobody dreamed they were sailing to war. The previous Saturday evening, March 20, Governor Hunt had told the captain of Endurance, Nick Barker, that some scrapmen had landed illegally on South Georgia. Endurance set off to arrest them, with her normal complement of 13 Marines reinforced by nine from the Falklands' own Landing Party 8901 and their commander, 22-year-old Lt Keith Mills.

Barker had been prophesying an Argentine invasion for months. He had heard word of it in dinner-party gossip in Buenos Aires the summer before; though when he tried to warn Defence Secretary John Nott during his leave in the autumn, his superiors had told him to shut his mouth. But not even Barker expected this crisis to erupt as it did.

They got to Grytviken on Wednesday March 24 and made contact with Steven Martin, commander of the British Antarctic Survey base there. The scrapmen were at Leith, 40 miles down the coast; but by now London was worried, so the Marines were told not to land. They waited, shadowed now by their Argentine counterpart, Bahia Paraiso. Then the crisis deepened, and on Wednesday March 31 Endurance landed her 23 Marines and, after dark, slid out of Grytviken, on orders to return to Stanley. An invasion was feared.

Ashore, Lt Mills set about fortifying his new domain. He had no clear orders – other than to protect the Survey people – but he assumed the worst. So next morning, Thursday April 1, the Survey team moved into the most solid building at Grytviken, the church, while Mills' party dug in on King Edwards Point, which controls the harbour mouth.

They were just in time. Around lunch, Bahia Paraiso sailed in, circled the bay and sailed out. The Marines kept their heads down. At 6.00 pm Paraiso's captain came on the radio: Steven Martin should stand by for an important message next day. At dawn next day, April 2, they heard the BBC World Service news of the invasion. They knew they were next.

Mills decided to announce his presence. When, around 7.30 am, Paraiso's captain came on with his 'important message' – which was that they were under Argentine rule and should assemble on the jetty – Mills replied briskly that there was a military presence here. This clearly disconcerted the Argentines. All day there was a lull. Meanwhile, 200 miles to the west, Endurance was crashing back to South Georgia as fast as her shaking hull could stand.

Halfway back to Stanley, Barker had been ordered to turn round. He was also given orders to pass on to Mills. As she drove into the seas, Endurance prepared for battle. Her solitary Bofors gun was uncovered; her orange Wasp helicopter was hastily sprayed black; and to its landing skids were

APRIL 3

'Sod that. I'm going to make their eyes water'

Lt Keith Mills, on being told he was to make only a show of resistance

It began, apparently, as a trivial incident on a vast and inhospitable island. It ended in a war costing hundreds of lives and, in all, billions of pounds. The view (*opposite*) from the mouth of Grytviken harbour in South Georgia shows both the scale of the island and the dereliction of the old whaling stations rusting around its coast. Few of the buildings at Grytviken are habitable. The church where scientists of the British Antarctic Survey sheltered during the battle is back right. The scrapmen were at Leith, three bays down from here. One reason why few at once spotted the crisis was that, when first asked to lower the Argentine flag they had raised over the ruined shed at Leith whaling station, the scrapmen did so (*top left*). But then in Buenos Aires the junta's line on the scrapmen seemed to harden. Or was it a plot right from the start?

fitted a pair of AS-12 anti-ship missile launchers – loaded.

Barker radioed Mills to pass on his orders. Mills was to resist only enough to prove Argentine aggression. Barker added his personal plea. 'This is only a piece of land,' he said. 'In three weeks, it will be swarming with naval ships and we'll easily get the islands back. But if you get killed, we can't get you back. So no heroics, just a show of resistance.' 'Sod that,' said young Keith Mills. 'I'm going to make their eyes water.'

When the Argentines moved into Grytviken harbour at 10.40 next morning, April 3, Mills and his men, in two hectic hours, shot down two helicopters and holed the corvette Guerrico with two anti-tank rockets and more than 1,000 rounds of machine-gun fire. Only when Guerrico limped back out of range and began to shell their positions – by which time they were also surrounded by 50 Argentine marines – did Mills and his men surrender. The Argentines could not believe there were only 23 of them.

Had Endurance been allowed to join the battle, Mills would probably have won. Endurance was only 40 miles from Grytviken when the Argentines moved in. (Barker too ignored orders, which were to stay 150 miles out.) Her Wasp helicopter had flown ahead of her and landed just behind the crest of the mountains over Grytviken. The two crew walked forward and peered over the edge at the action below. They begged to be allowed to join in with their rockets. 'We can sink her, we can sink her,' they radioed. But Barker had orders from London too. Endurance was on no account to get involved. Much to his personal regret, he had to refuse.

The two trips of Endurance to South Georgia as the crisis unfolded. On the first, when Endurance took him and his men down to the island to arrest the scrapmen, Lt Keith Mills was relaxed enough to pose (*below*) at the ship's wheel, a massively confident young soldier, also seen (*bottom*) with some of his Marines. The night before they went ashore, everyone aboard relaxed watching one of their favourites among the latest batch of video films to reach them: a recording of Ian Botham's innings in the Third Test. But on the second trip, as Endurance hurried back to give Mills his orders (and, Captain Nick Barker hoped, to help him) there was tension as the ship prepared to fight: pulling the cover off the Bofors gun and (*bottom right*) hurriedly spraying her Wasp helicopter black as camouflage.

The captain of Endurance, Nick Barker, is probably the world's most expert sailor in Antarctic waters. His years of skill saved Endurance. As the crisis deepened, Endurance was ordered to leave Grytviken and return to Stanley. But waiting outside Grytviken harbour was an Argentine naval vessel. Here Barker (*left*) is working out with navigator Bill Hurst (*centre*) how to slip out by night, without lights and with their radar off, to evade the Argentines. They did it by navigating through an ice-flow in the dark.

Lt Mills' own sketch map of the battle (*left*) with the same bay (*below* map) seen from above. Mills' men were dug in at (1). The Survey team were in the church at (2). The picture (*centre*) shows the scene inside the church. The Argentine corvette came by Mills in a wide circle (3) round the bay. The picture (*top right*) shows it as it came in view of men in the church tower. In this shot it is about at (4). On its way out, Mills' men hit it, then hit a Puma helicopter at (5), and an Alouette helicopter at (6). But by now enemy troops had landed at (7) and surrounded them. They surrendered to Captain Astiz (*below right*). (Three weeks later, Astiz was a captive, shipped to Britain amid charges he had tortured political prisoners. But as a PoW he had to be sent home.)

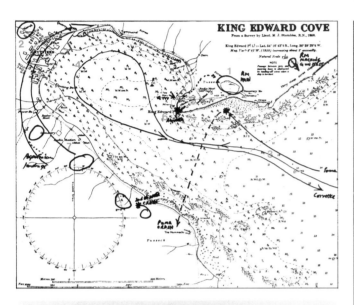

Endurance was now in grave danger from the Argentine warships at South Georgia, who were looking out for her. Barker saved the ship by playing a deadly game of hide-and-seek. Every night he took Endurance out into the pack-ice, edging her into the lee of an iceberg. He knew the Argentines would not venture into the ice-floes. By day, her red hull would have been visible to planes; so before dawn, Endurance would slip into some remote inlet or bay on South Georgia, and hide against the cliffs. Here she is in St Andrew's Bay. Then on April 6 Endurance was ordered to head north, to rendezvous with a secret British force already heading for South Georgia.

The fleet departs

They slid away on the morning tide, to scenes of emotion Britain had not witnessed since World War One. The quays of Portsmouth Dockyard were an array of flags and homemade banners with loving messages, carried mostly by the wives and mothers and girlfriends who waved through their tears. Slowly the carriers eased past, first the gleaming Invincible and then, looking her age, the Hermes. Somewhere a band was playing. Cockily at Invincible's bow, on the tip of its ski-jump flight deck, someone with a sense of occasion had perched a Harrier.

Over the next days and weeks, the Task Force gathered. The carriers and the assault ship Fearless were the first away, on April 5. The liner Canberra, carrying the Marines and some of the Parachute Regiment who would make up the assault force, followed from Southampton four days later, on Good Friday April 9. The other battalion of Paras sailed in Norland. The QE2, laden with Guards and Gurkhas, sailed on May 12. Gradually the armada assembled: more than 100 ships, from great liners to Hull trawlers, from the most lethal warships to British Rail ferries; 46 were requisitioned or chartered merchant ships. Some departures were grander than others. The emotions enveloping each were the same.

So was the backroom work. If it seemed a miracle that two carriers could sail just three days after the invasion, the secret answer was that the Navy had been preparing for weeks. In early March, when Argentine hysteria was

APRIL 5

'This is a sight I suppose most of us never thought to see in our lifetimes'

BBC reporter, as Hermes sailed from Portsmouth

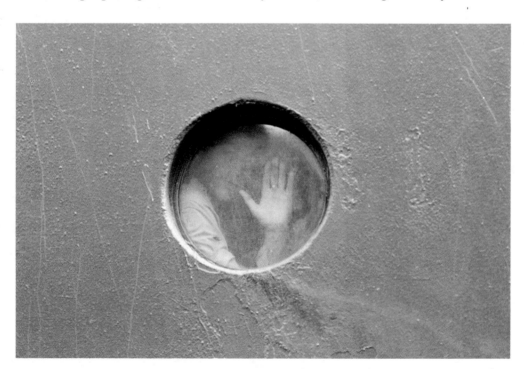

clearly rising, Ministry of Defence planners dusted off the file on how to send a Task Force into distant waters. Discreet meetings followed with companies like Sainsbury's and Esso, to check supplies. After the scrapmen landed on South Georgia, this work quickened. Finally, at a traumatic meeting in Mrs Thatcher's room in the House of Commons through the night of Wednesday, March 31 – when the Prime Minister at last faced the near-certainty of an invasion – the First Sea Lord, Sir Henry Leach, pledged that the Fleet would sail on the morning tide of Monday, April 5.

Somehow the troops were rounded up – many from leave, at least one

A corset is not recommended wear for chilly quaysides, but how often does a girl get to inflame three entire battalions of the British Army simultaneously? And if the troops displayed a chronic inability even to spell the name of the man whose soldiers they were sailing to fight (amply supplied with beer on the way, it seemed), that did not touch the poignancy of each private farewell amid this public throng.

from his wedding. ALL RANKS, 3RD PARACHUTE BATTALION. REPORT TO BARRACKS IMMEDIATELY read the sign chalked at main railway stations. 2 Para were due to go to Belize: all their kit was already at sea. The battalion was re-equipped from stock in 24 hours. And when the carriers sailed, they did so with scaffolding around Hermes' bridge, and with scores of dockyard workers still aboard. (Many, poignantly, had redundancy notices in their pockets.) None of that mattered. They sailed, as the Navy had promised, on the morning tide. They turned into the Solent, hulls shining in the haze. Then slowly, slowly they were gone.

Of course, politicians made capital out of the sailings: the Government to divert attention from the blunder of allowing the invasion in the first place; the dissenters to promote their wider causes. But emotions for once overwhelmed words; and the sight of Invincible in the Solent awakened historic memories.

Living under occupation

Having conquered the Falklands, the Argentines seemed confused about what to do with them – or with their inhabitants. President Galtieri arrived on the island to celebrate the triumph and to swear-in General Mario Benjamin Menendez as military governor. Menendez installed himself in Governor Hunt's old office, changing little except the flag by the desk and the portraits on the walls. But his rule was full-blown martial law. A stream of proclamations, regulations and edicts issued forth: insulting Argentina or its soldiery was particularly frowned upon. Curfews were instituted; driving on the right decreed. Menendez talked grandly of converting the schools to the Spanish language and curriculum. It was no way to win the hearts and minds of the islanders. Yet clearly that had been some part of the Argentines' intention. When British troops much later broke into containers beside one of the roads in Stanley, they found an Aladdin's Cave of video sets, tape recorders, all sorts of electronic goodies that the Argentines had evidently planned to distribute. But what use were video recorders to people who did not have television?

The Argentine Army intelligence officer who took over as police chief revealed to one local that they had files on about 500 islanders; and with some efficiency they deported one or two of the more influential. A handful more – mainly senior civil servants in the old administration – they packed off to Port Howard on West Stanley. On that level, they were well prepared. But their military preparations verged on fantasy. Men and machines poured on to the islands. But the numbers merely heightened what must have been nightmarish supply problems for Menendez – even allowing for the fact that, contrary to British claims, Stanley runway was never blocked.

For the islanders, the experience of occupation varied greatly. The sharpest contrast was of course between Stanley, which soon swarmed with troops, and the remoter settlements, whose contact might be limited to a few helicopter visits. The other distinctions were a matter of background. The expatriates, in the islands on contract for the British Government, the local administration or the Falkland Islands Company, almost to a man left with their families. But fewer than 25 of the native-born Falklanders quit. What more than half the residents of Stanley did do was to leave the city to stay with friends or relatives in the settlements. Conditions got pretty cramped in some communities, but food was never a problem: everyone had stocked up for the approaching winter. There seems little doubt that those who, for one reason or another, elected to stay in Stanley had the worst time – not because of Argentine brutality, simply the unremitting stress of living under armed occupation, and occupation by a horde of terrified, trigger-happy kids at that. Yet in Stanley could also be found the other extreme: a few middle-

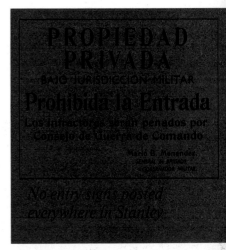

PROPIEDAD PRIVADA
BAJO JURISDICCION MILITAR
Prohibida la Entrada
Los infractores serán penados por Consejo de Guerra de Comando

Mario B. Menendez
GENERAL DE BRIGADA
GOBERNADOR MILITAR

No-entry signs posted everywhere in Stanley

The Falklands people looked on bewildered, at first frightened and then almost detached, as the Argentine military build-up continued. What the Argentines hoped to achieve with this row of armoured personnel carriers (*opposite*) is unclear. They would bog down uselessly in the soft peat which covers 80 per cent of the islands.

class people who did strike up wary acquaintanceships with the more civilised Argentine officers. That simply did not happen in the settlements. Out there, however – and with a humanity which did them credit – the islanders found it possible in their hearts to make a distinction between the officers, whom they disliked as arrogant, and the troops, for whom they often felt sorry.

As the build-up continued, the islanders watched it with a certain detachment. The first reaction to invasion had been intense gloom. But now everyone realised Mrs Thatcher was serious about re-taking the islands. So the islanders watched their letters being franked ISLAS MALVINAS and PUERTO ARGENTINA (Stanley's new name) in the same way that the Stanley shopkeepers looked upon the peso notes that the troops changed in their stores: as an aberration that would soon be righted, a bad dream from which they would wake – rather than as the profound change Argentina was proclaiming. Soon, the question for the islanders became, what would happen to them when the fighting started?

The Argentine Military Governor, General Mario Menendez, moved into the old office of Governor Hunt, changing only the flag by his desk and the portraits on the wall (*below*).

The Argentine build-up could continue at the pace it did because the runway at Stanley airport never closed. The dusk flight (*left*) was a daily one, even when the 'Total Exclusion Zone' was in force. The bombing raid by the Vulcan, though a fine logistical feat by the RAF, did not succeed, though at the time it looked dramatic (*below*). Meanwhile, the people tried to get on with their lives: (*bottom*) the doctor, Alison Bleaney, with young Emma, talks to Eileen Vidal at morning surgery in Stanley.

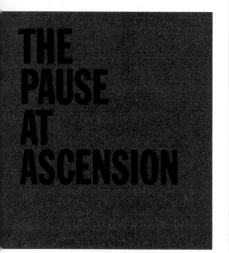

THE PAUSE AT ASCENSION

It was kept secret at the time, but the Task Force waited days at Ascension. Canberra's troops stayed two weeks. The Task Force had sailed so hurriedly that all its equipment was stowed in a muddle. While helicopters shifted gear between vessels, the men had the grind of endurance marches and the pleasure of prodigal weapons practice. (In one day, 3 Para's anti-tank platoon fired $37\frac{1}{2}$ *years'* worth of training rounds.) Meanwhile the Paras learnt how to clamber into landing craft, and the Marines were taught helicopter assaults, because nobody yet knew how the attack on the Falklands would be made. Ascension's baking heat was not the best preparation for icy Falklands weather, but it did give the tired troops a memorable time (each unit had an afternoon on the beach). Out of bounds on the peaks above were the masts of the US–British intelligence base, tuned now to Argentine military and diplomatic signals. Equally secret were the US Air Force flights into Ascension with supplies, including more modern air-to-air missiles for the Harriers.

In distinctly unmilitary orange lifejackets, the men of 2 Para return to their ship Norland after a hasty introduction to landing craft assaults.

Belying its name, Wideawake Airfield on Ascension is usually a somnolent place. But from early April, it teemed (*left*) with aircraft bringing men and supplies to the Task Force. On a few days it was, in its total of aircraft 'movements', the busiest airport in the world. On April 17, Admiral Sir John Fieldhouse, C-in-C Fleet and overall commander of the Task Force, flew in secret to Wideawake and thence on to Hermes for the key conference of the force's military commanders, to decide the question: how, precisely, are the Falklands to be retaken? And from here, on the night of April 30, the Vulcans, refuelled by Victors (*above*), flew south on their attempt, which contrary to stories at the time was totally unsuccessful, to bomb the Falklands' only runway at Port Stanley.

Gazing out one morning at the fleet stretched around him, the commanding officer of one unit remarked that it was like the old saying about the swan: 'graceful on the surface, but working like mad underneath'. And certainly the contrast is striking between Canberra's serenity as she sails into an evening shower (*below*) and the grim clutter of the Hermes' hangar deck (*right*), crammed with more Harriers than it had ever carried. More were stowed on deck.

The long voyage South

It was a limbo, neither peace nor war. Even as they sailed south, few in the Task Force could believe there would be fighting. And the fact that the ships cruised below their top speed and on occasion even sailed in a big circle – presumably to waste time while diplomacy was tried – added to the unreality. So the Marine band played a medley, of their own arranging, called South American Holiday. A titled young tank commander in the Blues & Royals was heard lamenting that he really didn't want to go to war with Argentina: all the best polo ponies came from there. And the journalists, inevitably, entertained each unit in turn to a lavish champagne party.

But the activity on Ascension had had a sobering effect. Then in the first four days of May a succession of news items changed the mood utterly: the bombing of Stanley runway; then the sinking of the Belgrano; then, shockingly, the instantaneous destruction of Sheffield. On Canberra, the unit

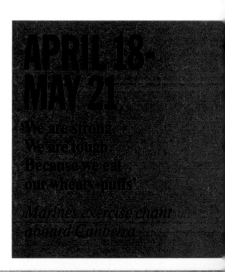

APRIL 18-
MAY 21

'We are strong,
We are tough,
Because we eat
our wheaty-puffs'

*Marines' exercise chant
aboard Canberra*

For the troops, the voyage brought dawn-to-dusk drills and training. So many men had entered the London Marathon run, which now of course they would miss, that the Task Force arranged a substitute marathon round the decks (*left*). But most of the training, as for these men of 40 Commando (*below*) was of the more traditional military sort.

commanders became preoccupied with the perils of an opposed landing. Folk-memories of Gallipoli run deep in the Services; and, besides, the officers were far from unanimously in favour of the expedition. 'Dying for Queen and Country is one thing,' a Marine officer remarked grimly. 'Dying for Mrs Thatcher is quite another.'

To the south, the carriers Hermes and Invincible were already at war, their Harriers trying to establish air superiority over the Falklands so the soldiers now approaching could land in safety. And though few knew it, British forces were already on the islands. On the night of May 1, 12 reconnaissance

'Cross-decking' the military called it: the seemingly endless process of sorting men and stores into the ships and order they would need to go into battle. So the helicopters clattered ceaselessly between the vessels of the Task Force. This Sea King (*below*) is lifting officers from Fearless after one of the last planning meetings.

patrols of the Special Air Service and Special Boat Squadron were helicoptered ashore from Hermes. Avoiding all contact with the islanders, the patrols began to spy out the enemy positions.

On May 18, the fleet slid into the 200-mile 'Total Exclusion Zone' around the Falklands. They could not linger there: the Argentine Air Force would surely find them when the weather cleared. But still the signal to land had not come. And even now not everyone was caught up in the drama. One Marine officer was ordered off the bridge of Fearless for inciting the officer on watch to look for seabirds rather than enemy aircraft. 'One must keep a sense of proportion about these things,' he protested.

The frigate Ardent ploughs through the South Atlantic (*right*). The troops hated the rough weather but the commanders blessed the cover it gave them from air attack. The Argentine submarines, seen as the other threat, never turned up. Ardent was later sunk, in the first day's air attacks at San Carlos Water.

As the Task Force neared the 'Total Exclusion Zone' the ships closed up, until – like Atlantic Conveyor and its escorting frigate (*left*) – they sailed in tight formation. The risk of air-raids grew and the gunners stood at post in their flash-masks (*below*). Signalling between ships was only by Aldis lamp now (*bottom*) with radio silence enforced.

LAS HEMOS
RECUPERADO
A COSTA DE SANGRE
ARGENTINA!
Sra M. THATCHER
COLECTIVIDAD

Politics and planning

APRIL-MAY

'I think we should sail into Stanley Harbour and just go Whap!'

One of Commando planning team aboard Fearless

The view from the balcony of the Presidential palace in Buenos Aires. The delirious crowds (with one banner from the Argentine AA and another reminding the world that the Falklands invasion had cost Argentine blood) would surely have swayed even a strong leader. And General Galtieri (*above*) was not that.

'We started out quite hopeful,' one of US Secretary of State Al Haig's assistants said later. 'Surely to God nobody was going to war over a bog. But the deeper we got, the more we saw the problem was intellectually insoluble.' Argentine determination was palpable. Tens of thousands thronged outside the Casa Rosada, the presidential palace in Buenos Aires, in a patriotic delirium. In Britain the crowds were mostly of the relatively few dissenters. But the opinion polls showed how deep feelings ran in Britain too – and, predictably, hardened as the human costs mounted. In the House of Commons in the wake of the invasion, Labour leader Michael Foot was more stridently bellicose than the Prime Minister. And the outrage in Mrs Thatcher's own Conservative ranks was caught by backbencher Edward du Cann, who dismissed problems of distance and logistics witheringly: 'I do not remember the Duke of Wellington whining about the Torres Vedras.'

The first casualty of this mood was the Foreign Secretary, Lord Carrington, who promptly and properly resigned. Defence Secretary John Nott only just survived. And Mrs Thatcher's room for negotiation was correspondingly limited. In Buenos Aires, meanwhile, the junta was paralysed. 'It's just 40 guys who spend all their time in the Casa Rosada keeping an eye on each other,' another US official lamented.

So while the three phases of peacemaking – first the effort through resolutions of the United Nations Security Council, then Secretary Haig's gruelling 'shuttle' between London and Buenos Aires, finally the mediation of the

Who was to blame for the failure of the British Government to foresee and forestall the invasion? The Foreign Secretary, Lord Carrington (*far left*) resigned; and indeed the Foreign Office dominates the Joint Intelligence Committee which had the job of assessing the evidence. Mrs Thatcher refused to accept the resignation of (*left*) Defence Secretary John Nott (though after the war he decided to quit politics). But more detailed allocation of blame awaited the report of the inquiry under Lord Franks.

new UN Secretary-General, Javier Perez de Cuellar – were complex and ingenious, they never really looked like solving the 'intellectually insoluble'. As that US official explained: 'Once Galtieri had invaded, there was no concession Mrs Thatcher could make big enough to compensate him for withdrawing again – except the concession of sovereignty, which was the one thing *she* could not give and survive.'

'We reminded the junta of the British fleet,' that official said. 'But they refused to believe it would get beyond Ascension. "How can they hope to mount an assault so far from their own base and so close to ours?" was their attitude.' That was precisely the question now engaging the British military commanders sailing south with the Task Force.

OPERATION CORPORATE, the codename for the Task Force, needed time to mount an assault on the Falklands. Time to establish air superiority; to collect intelligence about Argentine forces on the islands; time to organise and train. But Mrs Thatcher was calling for results.

In overall command of the Task Force was Rear Admiral John 'Sandy' Woodward, an intellectual submariner. Then there was Commodore Michael Clapp, whose job was 'amphibious warfare'. The teeth were the Marines of 3 Commando Brigade – reinforced by 2 Para and 3 Para – under Brigadier Julian Thompson. So it fell to Thompson's staff to work out how to translate political will into military action. The planners wanted raids. London decreed a landing. Then the question was: where?

Direct on Port Stanley? Mrs Thatcher was said to favour that. But it was ruled out: too many Argentines, and probably mines in the bay. (And an Entebbe-style airborne landing was also rejected, somewhat to the SAS's regret.) What about a bay *near* Stanley? (Cow Bay and Uranie Bay – see the map on pages 48/49 – were possible sites.) The risk of Argentine counter-attack before the landings were consolidated was ruled to be too great.

So where? Admiral Woodward favoured a site on Lafonia (not too far from Stanley) or somewhere on *West* Falklands where he could lay down a landing strip for Phantom fighter-bombers. But either site posed insuperable problems for the land forces.

Gradually, from a list of 21 possible bays on East Falklands given to the planners by a Marine major, Ewen Southby-Tailyour, who had been a Falklands enthusiast since serving there in the late 1970s, a list of eight possible sites was sifted. From these, San Carlos Water began to emerge.

Emotions were running too high for compromise. Was the Argentine pop Press (*left*) responding to the emotions or fanning them? Either way, Secretary Haig's shuttle efforts (and somehow, *top*, he made time in Buenos Aires for a game of tennis) had as little impact as protests (*above*) in Britain.

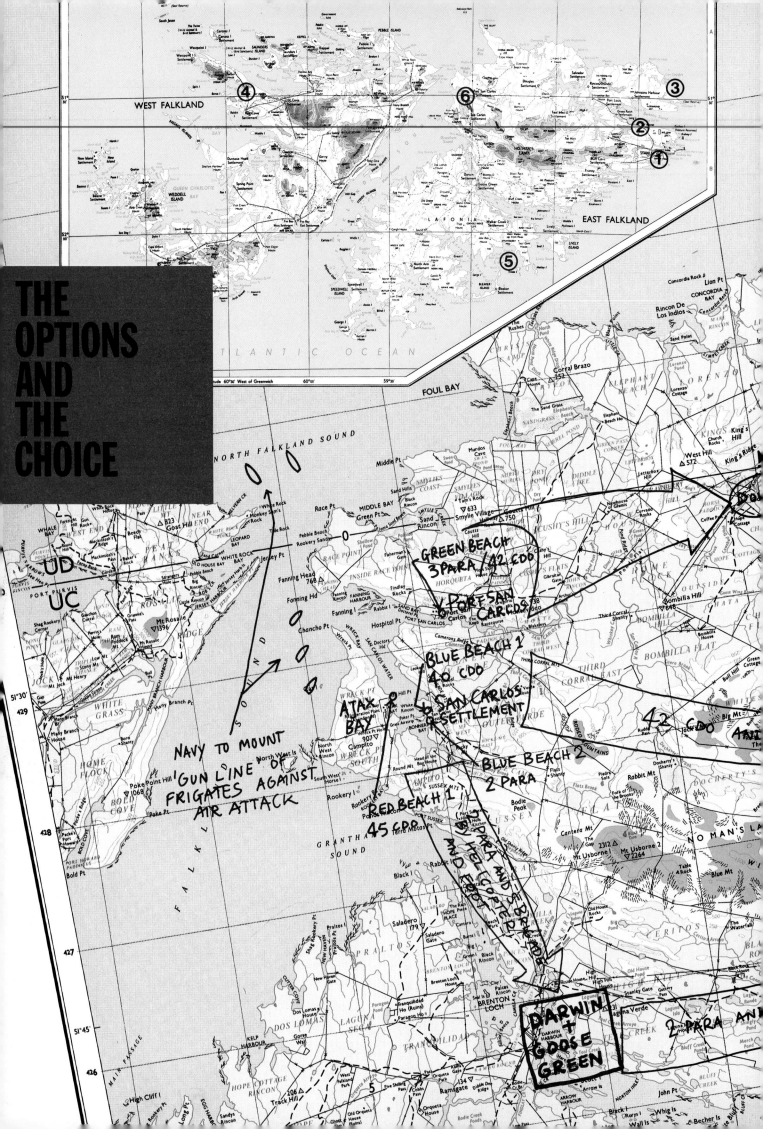

THE OPTIONS AND THE CHOICE

Landing options: see map (*left*)

1 **Stanley:** Enemy HQ. Quick kill. Mrs Thatcher's favourite. But strongly held. Risk to civilians.

2 **Uranie Bay:** Stanley only 25 miles. Thompson interested but Gunners fear counter-attack.

3 **Cow Bay:** Far enough from Stanley to give time for build-up. Thompson's favourite.

4 **Port North:** Possible airstrip site? Woodward's favourite. Too far from Stanley, Thompson says.

5 **Low Bay:** Good beach, easy landing. Woodward's 2nd choice. But flat. Thompson fears air attack.

6 **San Carlos:** Sheltered landing sites. Hills for Rapier batteries. Dominates both islands. 65 miles from Stanley. Woodward's 3rd choice. Thompson's 2nd. The compromise.

The scale of the place is awesome. *Above:* A Marine recce patrol high over Leith harbour, with Endurance dwarfed below them. *Right:* a patrol on a saddle of rock with Mount Paget rising 9,600 ft behind them. *Far right:* Major Guy Sheridan, leader of the South Georgia mission, is on the left.

Retaking South Georgia

Mrs Thatcher wanted results. Operation Paraquet, codename for the retaking of South Georgia, supplied them – just. The opening British shot in the campaign, the return to that island of ice 800 miles beyond the Falklands, nearly ended in catastrophe. The enemy was the weather.

Major Guy Sheridan of 42 Commando had been an obvious choice to lead the mission. Arctic explorer and ski-racing champion, he led the 110 highly-motivated men of 42's M Company: the 'Mighty Munch', they called themselves. When 42 left their barracks outside Plymouth on April 8, M Company stayed hidden in the gym. The men were forbidden to phone their wives. Two days later, they flew to Ascension and sailed south on the destroyer Antrim and the auxiliary Tidespring. Also on board were 60 men of the SAS and the Special Boat Squadron. Two days out, they made a rendezvous with Endurance, which had sailed up from South Georgia carrying scientists of the island's British Antarctic Survey team. As the three-ship armada headed south, the scientists briefed the SAS and SBS on Argentine strengths and locations, and on possible reconnaissance and assault routes. Sheridan decided to send in SAS and SBS recce parties. But as they set off on April 21, a 50 mph snow storm blew.

APRIL 25

'Have much to tell you when we rejoin...'

Signal from Major Guy Sheridan to Fearless after the operation

The SAS patrol helicoptered on to the Fortuna Glacier, to look down on the forces at Leith harbour. But the blizzard rose to 100 knots and by next morning the SAS men were in real physical peril. A helicopter from Antrim rescued them but then crashed in the gale. So did a second. Miraculously a third, grossly overloaded with 17 men, made it back to Antrim but had to crash-land on the heaving deck. Next day the SAS went back in five rubber dinghies. Two of their engines failed. One drifting boat was retrieved. The other made landfall on the last tip of South Georgia before the open sea. The SAS men hid on the rocks for a week.

As the blizzard rages, the SAS men try to salvage their kit from the crashed Wessex. *Inset:* the Wessex was no more than a black splinter in the vastness of the Fortuna Glacier.

At last the expedition, reinforced now by Plymouth and Brilliant, struck lucky. A Lynx helicopter from Brilliant spotted the Argentine submarine Santa Fe on the surface, bringing reinforcements into Grytviken, and shot it up with rockets and machine-gun. Most of M Company were still 200 miles back on Tidespring, but Sheridan realised he had to attack at once, before the men from that battered submarine could deploy. Rounding up 45 SAS and SBS men and 60 marines from Antrim, he landed on the other side of the mountain behind Grytviken, while Antrim and Plymouth opened up with their 4.5 inch guns. The Argentines promptly surrendered.

Top left: the HQ party in the march on Grytviken rest on the last ridge above the harbour. They looked over to see the Argentines flying white flags. *Below left:* The assault party prepares to cram into Antrim's Wessex after news of Santa Fe has reached them. *Centre:* The Union Jack flies over Grytviken once more, along with the emblem of Sheridan's M Company. The Argentine garrison along the coast at Leith was disposed to fight on, but was dissuaded by the sight of Antrim offshore. *Below:* Santa Fe, listing badly, just made it to Grytviken jetty. *Bottom:* that evening, Captain Nick Barker of Endurance (left) talks with Captain Brian Young of Antrim.

South Georgia's recapture had an air of derring-do. But the torpedoing of the cruiser Belgrano brought a grim realisation that this war could be bloody. A British nuclear sub, Conqueror, had tailed the 10,650 ton cruiser and two escort destroyers for a day as they zig-zagged round the

MAY 2: THE SINKING OF BELGRANO

southern edge of the 'Total Exclusion Zone', heading east. By next dawn the ships could be up by Britain's two aircraft carriers, which were south-east of the Falklands. Told of this, the War Cabinet ordered Conqueror to fire. Two torpedoes hit the port side of the ship shortly before dusk on May 2. 368 of Belgrano's 1,100 crew were killed.

As the ship began to list heavily the crew took to the dinghies (*left*), one of them taking his camera and filming the final minutes of the cruiser (*above*). But then a high sea blew up, and it was more than 24 hours before the survivors could be picked up. Many of the wounded died of exposure in the dinghies.

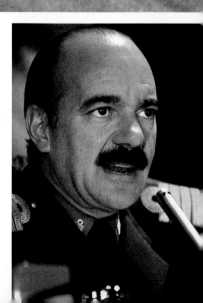

Belgrano's captain, Comandante Hector Bonzo (*far left*), claimed later the Belgrano had been heading back to port when it was hit. But the fact was that the two nations were at war. And as they absorbed the scenes of tearful reunion with the Belgrano's survivors, the question was: what next?

MAY 4: THE SINKING OF SHEFFIELD

The British feared that the Argentine navy would retaliate for Belgrano with a submarine attack. But shortly after lunch on May 4, the Royal Navy learnt to its cost how inadequate its defences were against the latest generation of supersonic sea-skimming anti-ship missiles. (A major failure: the Soviet Naval Air Force has, as its main weapons, low-flying cruise-missiles.) The Task Force was south-east of the Falklands, with Sheffield on picket duty 30 miles west of the carriers. Two Argentine Super-Etendards, each carrying beneath its wing a French Exocet missile, set out from the Rio Gallegos air base towards the British fleet. They bobbed over the horizon for only a few seconds, just long enough to feed bearings of the British ships into the mini-computer each missile carries. Then they fired. One Exocet headed towards Sheffield at the speed of sound, skimming 6 feet above the waves. The men on watch spotted the missile only about four seconds before it struck them.

The missile blast wiped out the ship's Operations Room, its nerve centre (*below*). Within seconds Sheffield was a blazing wreck (*above*). Only the discipline of its 280 crew kept the death toll down to 20. Technicians from its French makers had helped the Argentines fit Exocet (*right*), though it is unclear if the French Government, which told Britain they had not been fitted, knew this.

Sheffield's captain, John Salt (*above*), later described the effect of the missile: 'It was 15 to 20 seconds before the whole of the working area of the ship was filled with black, acrid, pungent smoke ... On the upper deck you could feel the heat of the deck through your feet with your shoes on. The superstructure was steaming. The paint on the ship's side was coming off. Around the initial area where the missile penetrated the hull was glowing red, it was white hot and red hot.' As the casualties were flown on to Hermes (*left*) the survivors waiting to come off Sheffield stood on the ship's foredeck, singing 'You've got to look on the bright side of life'.

The men of 42 Commando go
ashore. Some still wear berets:
there were too few helmets.
And note the size of the pack
on the right. *Right*: The
landing craft dock in Fearless.
The rear doors closed and the
dock drained to carry the craft
during passage.

Landing at San Carlos

PALPAS was the codeword the Task Force was waiting for: the signal from London to land. The mediation efforts of UN Secretary General Perez de Cuellar finally collapsed in New York on May 18. For 24 hours Mrs Thatcher's War Cabinet brooded. Then at 11.25 am on May 20, Brigadier Julian Thompson marched into a meeting of his staff on Fearless, waving a message: PALPAS. 'Gentlemen,' he said, 'we go.'

'Go' meant landing 2,400 Marines and Paras at four points around San Carlos Water before dawn next day. The operation had been minutely planned. Eleven ships, led by Fearless and Intrepid, were to sail straight for Port Stanley as if making a direct assault. After dark, the convoy would veer right and skirt round to Falkland Sound, the channel between East and West Falklands, and so into San Carlos Water. First ashore would be the SBS with a Spanish-speaking Marine, Captain Roderick Bell. His task was to negotiate the silent surrender of an Argentine patrol identified on Fanning Head, the promontory rising to the north of San Carlos Water. Then the SBS would guide in the landing craft.

Of course, it did not work quite like that. First the weather changed. It had blown a Force 8 gale for days: the troops groaned but their commanders were pleased: low cloud and heavy rain kept enemy aircraft at bay. But as the armada slid into San Carlos Water and the landing craft bobbed beside their mother ships, the sea was flat and a myriad of stars shone in the cold and brilliant sky.

Then the patrol on Fanning Head refused to surrender, and the navy opened up with 4.5 inch guns. Bang went the silent landing, though as a Para sergeant remarked: 'The noise does get the adrenalin going.' Finally a trooper in 2 Para slipped – clambering in full kit from Norland into the landing craft alongside, he fell and broke his pelvis – and with him slipped the timetable. With 40 Commando, 2 Para were to be the first ashore; but by the time 2 Para pushed off the operation was running an hour late.

The landings themselves had elements of fantasy. Put out to find they had to wade through waist-high water to the beach, the first Para units were further disconcerted to be greeted there by apparitions in white cowls. 'Bloody hell, they're nuns,' one Para officer said, only to realise they were SBS men in anti-flash hoods. He introduced himself and his men. 'We're 2 Para,' he said. 'We're invading.' At least 2 Para were ashore. When 3 Para finally reached their objective, Port San Carlos Settlement – their first landing craft had broken down – they found no shelving beach. As dawn broke over the Falklands, it revealed a landing craft full of black-faced soldiers disconsolately chugging up and down, while a man in the bow prodded with a long pole to find the shallows. Behind them, in full daylight now, splashed the

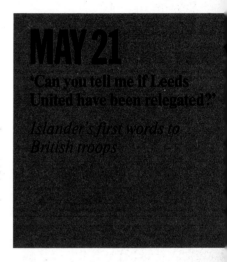

next wave, 42 Commando. As their CO, Lt Col. Nick Vaux, waded ashore, he joked: 'It's all so undignified.'

It was as well, perhaps, that the spectators were in the main the people of the settlement. They proved a phlegmatic bunch. The CO of 40 Commando, Lt Col. Malcolm Hunt, knocked proudly on the door of the settlement manager's house. 'Oh,' said the man, opening it, 'we thought you'd turn up sooner or later.' Another welcomed the Paras into his home with the question uppermost in his mind: 'Can you tell me if Leeds United have been relegated?' 'Not exactly cool,' Hunt said of their reception later. 'But muted.'

Apart from the flurry at Fanning Head, the Argentine response was – in the first hours – equally muted. Yet in this bright morning sunshine, amid the eerie calm of this bustling military scene, with the green hills enfolding the great ships in the bay, for all the world like some vast Scottish sea loch, the British land forces learned they were at war. A party of 43 Argentine Marines had withdrawn from Port San Carlos before dawn, leaving behind kit and quantities of rubbish. Sitting now on a hilltop barely a mile back from the water, they opened up with a machine-gun on two Gazelle helicopters that were escorting a Wessex as it lifted to high ground a Rapier anti-aircraft missile battery. Three of the four men in the Gazelles were killed.

For the troops, like these of 40 Commando (*above*), the prospect of action was a relief after so long on ship. But not all landings were so textbook as that by 42 Commando (*right*).

The radio operator of a 42
Commando patrol cuts
through the dawn mist of that
first day (*left*). A Wessex goes
in for the first British casualty
on land: a man whose pack
was so heavy he broke his back
stepping into a small ditch.
And (*below*) one of 40
Commando feels exposed on
the open plain as the
ubiquitous helicopter chugs by
on the horizon.

'It's such open country,' one CO said with a sigh. 'You stand out like a turd on a billiard table.' But the commanders reckoned they only needed eight hours grace. If they could get the guns and missile batteries into place that first day, then Rapiers on the hillsides and howitzers in the valleys would protect them from the attacks they knew must be coming. So from dawn the helicopters ceaselessly clattered overhead, ferrying the guns and ammunition, stores and vehicles across the water from the ships. Meanwhile the units ashore tried to find cover, dug defensive positions, and put out their first patrols into this astonishingly lovely landscape.

3 Para digging in at San Carlos
Settlement. The flurry conceals
the real skill. The object is to
make a trench blend into the
landscape. You cut turf off an
area, pile it to one side, then
dig the trench in the middle of
the cleared area, dumping your
spoil on the bare earth around
you. Next you roof half the
trench. Scrounge fence posts or
corrugated iron for a ceiling,
but you have in your pack a
special plastic sheet, usually
called a kip. Anchor this with
the rods also in your pack: it
will bear two feet of earth.
Pack the spoil neatly as a
parapet and thick roof.
Arrange the turves back on the
top of the whole and you have
a trench almost invisible from
100 yards which will also give
you shelter from air-burst
shells and bombs. The padres'
trenches on the Falklands
could be distinguished by the
small crosses on their roofs.
The 42 Commando padre,
Albert Hempinstall, dug at
Port San Carlos a trench so
commodious and with such a
big cross on it, that it was
known as The Cathedral.

D-Day morning at San Carlos was rather like Bank Holiday Monday at Blackpool. Troops dug in feverishly. Small boys piled peat round the trenches and begged berets as trophies. (The Task Force lost dozens in the campaign.) Girls served soup in buckets and tea in Jubilee mugs. And like new arrivals at a seaside resort, the British negotiated beds for the night. Troops camped in the sheep-shearing sheds, officers in the social club. One journalist commandeered a greenhouse – not a good air-raid shelter – and another camped in an (empty) chicken-coop. At midday, the tents came ashore and a canvas city sprang up. The British had arrived.

Sergeant-Major Laurie Ashbridge of 3 Para gets a cup of tea at San Carlos Settlement (*above*) yet already it is the camera which gets the attention. But the Argentine marines had only just left, as this resident is pointing out to another Para (*right*).

'We reflect upon the absurdity of it all,' one reporter wrote later. 'We have come 8,000 miles, crossed half the world, to liberate a place that looks like western Scotland, where the people speak with Devon accents and give the children names like Heather, Jenny, Tony, Keith and Ken.' It was a crisp introduction to the incongruities which were the hallmark of the Falklands war. But within hours the first patrols were bringing back prisoners: young men whose wild eyes and alien features only demonstrated further the fact that, whatever the historical arguments, the Falklands and their people were a world away from the Argentines who claimed them.

Sergeant Watson of 3 Para leads in the first prisoner (*right*): a conscript who is still wearing the British Marines jersey he looted from Moody Brook Barracks after the Argentine invasion.

What the Argentine pilots saw (*below*) as they came in to attack. This shot was taken from a helicopter at dusk on May 21, after hours of attack by more than 70 enemy planes. It shows the view from Falkland Sound south-east into San Carlos Water, their attack route that day. In the centre is Argonaut, which had taken two bombs on its stern and had no steering. In all, five of the eight warships stationed at the approaches to San Carlos Water the first day were hit. Two, Broadsword and Brilliant, were armed with Sea Wolf, designed to destroy low-flying aircraft. The Navy's luck was that three of the bombs did not explode, because the Argentine armourers, seen (*right*) fusing a bomb and writing a rude message on it – addressed to Prince Andrew, actually – did not set the fuses correctly.

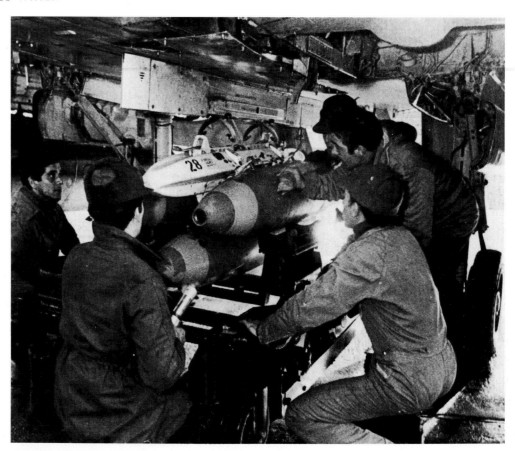

Battle of San Carlos Water

The Argentines had victory in their grasp. They threw it away. Within hours of the landings the Argentine pilots proved they had the power to inflict the worst amphibious disaster since Gallipoli. The roll of naval casualties tells the tale. **May 21,** the landings: Ardent (sunk); Argonaut (badly damaged); Antrim, Brilliant, Broadsword (hit by bombs which did not explode). **May 23:** Antelope (sunk by late-detonating bomb); Glasgow (hit by bomb which did not explode). **May 24:** Sir Galahad and Sir Lancelot (hit by bombs which did not explode: Galahad is abandoned for a time). **May 25:** Coventry (sunk); Atlantic Conveyor (destroyed by Exocet). Add to that the later casualties. **June 8:** Plymouth (hit, just survived). **June 12:** Glamorgan (hit by Exocet, survived). And of course the first loss: **May 4:** Sheffield (sunk by Exocet). It is the catalogue of a near-disaster.

The Task Force survived for two main reasons. The Argentine pilots, in

MAY 21-25

'Mmm, it's going to be a day to remember'

Senior Naval Officer on Canberra after the first air raid

their Skyhawks and Mirages, were superbly skilful and wincingly brave. But they evidently did not bother to talk to their armourers, the men who loaded and fused their bombs. The bombs were fused to explode after not less than 150–200 yards of free flight. But the pilots were launching them barely 50 yards from the ships. The fuses – basically, propellers which as they turn wind in a firing-pin – never wound up. The second reason, revealed by two pilots shot down and interrogated, was that instead of going for the vital targets, the supply ships – notably Canberra that first day – and the two amphibious assault ships, Fearless and Intrepid, the pilots had stupidly been ordered to attack the warships first. 'I would say that where the grace of God comes in,' Major-General Moore reflected later, 'is that on the first days in San Carlos the pilots went for the escorts and not the amphibious ships, for that might have stopped us altogether.'

Framed by bomb splashes (*above*) Norland gets under way to escape out to sea late on May 21, after her cargo, the men of 2 Para, had gone ashore. On her left is the support ship Stromness; to her right is the assault ship Intrepid. *Far left*: Inside the nerve centre of the Task Force that afternoon, the Amphibious Operations Room on board Fearless, where the fleet's air and sea defence was coordinated. This shot was taken during the battle. Most of those you see are radio operators. Each row – the two facing each other at the centre bank, and the row at the wall – are in touch with different groups of forces. The man standing with his back to the camera is the officer on duty, who is trying to cope with the crisis. The navy's defences were overwhelmed by waves of Skyhawks and Mirages. Ardent (*left*) took two 1,000 lb bombs on her stern and then another seven later. Yarmouth is alongside trying to help, but in vain.

The explosion and sinking of Antelope. After the attacks on May 21, there was a lull. The British pulled almost every ship out of San Carlos Water the first night. But on Sunday May 23 they came back in: supplies had to be unloaded. The Argentine planes attacked again: so low the pilot clipped the mast of Antelope while dropping two 500 lb bombs into her. They did not explode, but crashed down into the engine room. As it was being defused, one detonated. Her back broken, Antelope sank.

There is controversy about the performance of British anti-aircraft missiles. The Rapier (*above*) which is chasing a Mirage across the page, was effective, but took hours to set up, did not take kindly to the voyage and, being optically sighted, could not be used at night. (The radar-guided version only arrived later; until it did the British feared lest the Argentines start night attacks.) Sea Dart (shown *right*, going up from Exeter) worked against high-flying aircraft. (This one shot down a Lear jet whose passengers and purpose were never identified.) But Sea Dart did not work against low-level attacks. And it took vital seconds to switch from one incoming target to another. (Over the route the pilots flew, San Carlos Water was about two miles long. They covered its length in less than 18 seconds.) The hand-held Blowpipe was widely regarded as unsatisfactory. 'Like trying to shoot pheasants with a drainpipe,' was Brigadier Thompson's verdict. Even when an operator could track a plane, the missile itself could not catch it. (Blowpipe would be better against aircraft coming straight at you, if you had the nerve to stand and fire it.) Sea Wolf *was* a success against low-level attacks, but could defend only the ship firing it, no others. (The SAS, by mysterious means, acquired the excellent US-made Stinger hand-held missile for *their* protection.)

Spot the Mirage. Just how low the pilots flew can be seen in these pictures. The Mirage passing alongside Fearless (*left*) can just be spotted in front of her mast, level with her funnel. Another (*below left*) is not quite so low as it passes over supply ship Sir Bedivere. The Super-Etendard could launch Exocets from this height, and the missile would then track in at six feet or so over the waves. Atlantic Conveyor (*opposite below*, filmed later by a Harrier's cameras) was a casualty of Exocet on May 25, the last day of sustained attack. (Coventry was bombed and sunk the same day.) The pilots, who saw Conveyor only as a big blip on their radar screens, thought it was an aircraft carrier. So it was. Some Harriers used to 'park' on her big deck overnight. The loss of Conveyor's cargo was a savage blow to the Task Force. The three big troop-lifting Chinook helicopters aboard were to have ferried the British forces forward across the island. A fourth Chinook survived because it was flying at the time of the attack. The Wessex helicopters also lost would have flown up artillery and ammunition. Without them, the troops had to walk and the final battles took much longer to prepare. But at least Conveyor absorbed two Exocet missiles, saving the aircraft carriers.

THE SURGEONS' WAR

'Welcome to the Red & Green
Life Machine' said a sign
painted on the old meat
refrigeration plant at Ajax
Bay, on San Carlos Water.
Red & Green because Para
(red beret) and Naval
Commando (green) surgeons
worked there together in two
makeshift operating theatres.
Four surgeons, three
anaesthetists and a back-up
team of 100 nurses and
orderlies, working in shifts
round the clock as the
wounded were flown in by
'casevac' (casualty evacuation)
helicopter. Their achievements
were extraordinary: 202 major
operations (plus 108 done
elsewhere on the islands), more
than a third of them on
Argentine prisoners.
Everybody, except two gravely
injured, who got to Ajax Bay
alive, left alive for Canberra or
the hospital ship Uganda.
They worked through air raids,
sometimes sheltering under the
operating table. After one raid,
two 1000 lb bombs lodged
unexploded, one in a wall and
one in a ceiling. The team
covered them with sandbags –
and worked on.

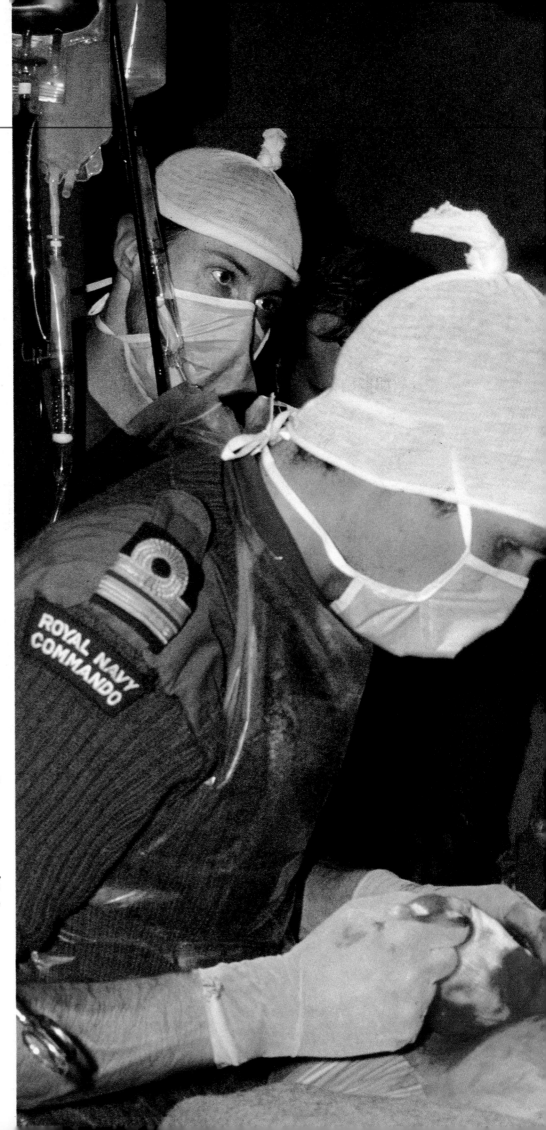

Picking up one of the first Argentine casualties.

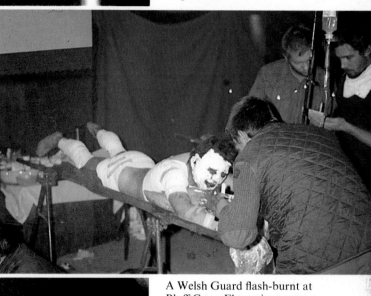

A Welsh Guard flash-burnt at Bluff Cove: Flamazine cream saved his face.

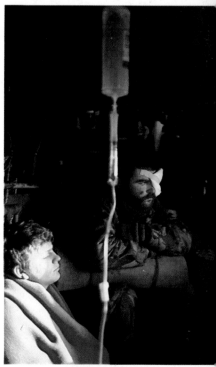

As the wounded were flown in from battle, a saline drip countered blood loss.

Battle for Goose Green

To the Commander, Argentine Forces, Goose Green
From the Commander, British Forces, Goose Green Area
MILITARY OPTIONS

We have sent a PoW to you under a White Flag of truce to convey the following military options:

1. That you surrender your force to us by leaving the township, forming up in a military manner, removing your helmets and laying down your weapons. You will give prior notice of this intention by returning the PoW under the White Flag, with him briefed as to the formalities, no later than 0830 hours local time.

2. You refuse in the first case to surrender and take the inevitable consequences. You will give prior notice of this intention by returning the PoW without his White Flag, although his neutrality will be respected, no later than 0830 hours local time.

3. In any event, and in accordance with the terms of the Geneva Conventions and the laws of war, you shall be held responsible for the fate of any civilians in Goose Green and we, in accordance with the laws, do give you prior notice of our intention to bombard Goose Green.

Signed C. Keeble
Commander, British Forces, Goose Green Area
29/5/82

MAY 28-29

'I've never been in anything like this before'

Robert Fox, BBC

'Neither have I'

Lt Col. 'H' Jones

When the soldiers of 2 Para entered Goose Green, they unlocked the doors of the community hall in which 114 local people had been locked for a month by the Argentines. The women at once made big pots of tea with lashings of sugar and gave it to the Paras in Jubilee and Royal Wedding mugs. Small children went among them offering slices of cake and biscuits; and someone found them packs of cigarettes. Slowly the exhausted men relaxed. It was dark in the hall, but Company Sergeant-Major Jed Peatfield (*opposite*) was standing in the light of a window. On the wall of the community centre hung a calendar with a view of a Cotswold village.

The prisoner went forward with the message in the early hours of May 29, down the long bare slope into Goose Green. Around the track as he walked the moorland surface was blotched by the craters of the withering Argentine artillery fire which had cleared the Paras off the slope all afternoon – and could as easily do so again, come the dawn. It was bitterly cold. Men huddled together on the crest of the hill and shivered, or tried to find room in the hot embers of the gorse hedge, still burning from the high explosive which had battered those fighting along its length. They wondered what the morning would bring. Everyone knew about the 114 civilians locked in Goose Green community centre. An hour after first light, the PoW emerged from the settlement below them. To their inexpressible relief, he was carrying a white flag. The Argentines had surrendered. One of the most remarkable feats of small arms in the history of the British Army, 2 Para's battle for Darwin and Goose Green, had ended in victory.

Myths already encrust the battle. *Myth No. 1* is that it was unnecessary, a sideshow. The truth is that the garrison at Goose Green was the crack 12th Regiment, the Argentines' strategic reserve and mobile reaction force. So long as it remained there, within march of San Carlos, the British bridgehead was under threat – a threat which had to be eliminated. *Myth No. 2* is that the operation went ahead only at London's insistence. In fact, London initially disapproved of the plan. On May 23, two days after landing, 2 Para's CO, Lt Col. Jones, emerged from a planning meeting aboard Intrepid with a timetable: the attack on Goose Green was to be on May 25. But next day, on the evening of May 24, the operation was cancelled; one reason, 2 Para's log records, was that 'the plan was not favoured in London.' But its military necessity could not be denied; and at noon on May 26, to 2 Para's considerable relief, the attack was reinstated. That evening, they set off from Sussex Mountain. *Myth No. 3* is that the BBC then leaked word of the plan to the Argentines. The BBC World Service did report, early on May 27, speculation in the British press that Goose Green had fallen; this in turn had been fed by gossip at the Ministry of Defence. By now, 2 Para were camped at Camilla Creek House, their jumping-off point for the attack, and Lt Col. Jones was

The Battle for Darwin and Goose Green, drawn from 2 Para's own map: a night-attack down a narrow isthmus ran into a superbly-sited line of Argentine bunkers stretching right across it. In the gruelling daylight battle which followed, 2 Para had also to endure heavy Argentine shelling, directed on to them by the Argentine observation post over the water to the east. The solid black lines of advance become dotted at the point each company had reached by dawn. The Paras attacked down each coast: B Company down the west coast, A Company down the east. Each ran into the defence-line stretching across from Darwin; and two separate battles developed one on each coast. It was in A Company's attack on the east that Lt Col. 'H' Jones was killed. The circle by the defence line shows the spot. A few yards from

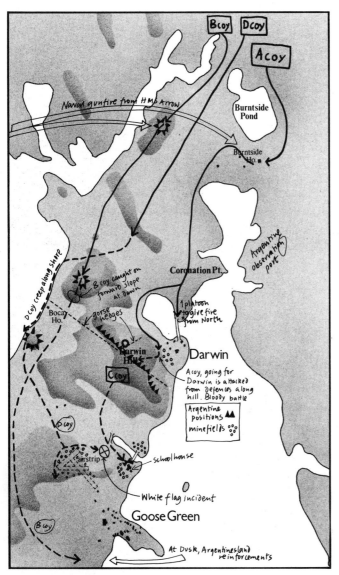

there the Paras had their medical post, where many of the pictures you see were taken. On the west coast B Company, pinned down by fire from the hill south of Boca House, were helped by D Company, which crept round the flank. With the defence line pierced, the Paras by nightfall had moved into position round Goose Green. The last Argentine strongpoint before Goose Green, the schoolhouse to its north, was demolished in the last battle of the day. It was as a platoon of D Company was moving up to join this assault that its lieutenant and its sergeant were shot while taking the surrender of an Argentine position flying the White Flag. At dusk, Argentine helicopters landed 150 reinforcements. But it was too late. Soon after dawn the Argentines surrendered.

Before the battle: *pages 82–83* show men of 2 Para leaving their positions on Sussex Mountain overlooking San Carlos Water at dusk, May 26. They knew they were going into battle, so they took no sleeping bags and only two days rations. The first stop south, Camilla Creek House, was reached by dawn. As they dug in, a squad out ahead brought back four prisoners, two of them wounded. While they were treated (*above left*) the other two, questioned, gave information about the forces at Goose Green. The 2 Para CO, Lt Col. 'H' Jones (*left*) drinking tea as a prisoner awaits interrogation, was pleased by this coup. (One oddity: all the Argentine patrol had as supplies was a big tub of margarine.) Towards dusk, the officers gathered (*top*) for Jones' O (Orders) Group. Grinning at the camera is the Adjutant, Captain David Wood, who was to be killed with Jones. They sat round him (*above*) as Jones, in dun anorak, gave his plan of battle, including the bad news they could take only two mortars, as they could not carry shells for more. Why 2 Para were not given more artillery support (and helicopters to lift the shells) is a mystery.

Daylight found them pinned down under accurate mortar and artillery fire. Some Paras took advantage of the minutest folds of land. Lance Corporal Peter Carroll of HQ Company rolls his own (*right*) while prisoners are processed. This is on the way to Coronation Point. Others dug hasty foxholes against blast: that below took eight minutes. 'I was really trying,' the man said. The mortar troop (*bottom*) was also trying: to give return fire. But they were short of shells and with each recoil the mortar base-plate dug into the peat, so ruining the aim. You can see behind this mortar the empty ammunition boxes that they filled with peat and rammed down to make foundations for the base-plates. Up ahead the medical post (*below right*) was coping with the first wave of Para wounded. It was right at the front line, tucked into a re-entrant, or fold, at the rear of Darwin Hill and just behind the gorse where the Paras were pinned down by the Argentine defences. The map on page 84 shows this.

furious when he heard the news. But in truth it told the Argentines nothing they did not know. The two reasons, apart from London's disfavour, why the attack had previously been cancelled are recorded in 2 Para's log as being that '(1) it was suspected the Argentines knew of our intentions; (2) their artillery [at Goose Green] had been enhanced.' (This assessment was later confirmed by Argentine prisoners.) *Myth No. 4* is that faulty intelligence failed to predict enemy strength. In fact the presence of 12th Regiment was known, also its likely numbers. Intelligence did *not* predict the hundreds of 'extras' – naval, Marine and HQ elements – who were there but played little part in the battle. As to the enemy's positions: through May 27, eight men from C Company went up from Camilla Creek House to high ground to spy out the defences. They did a superb job, mapping enemy strongpoints as far south as Boca Hill. (See the map on page 84.) On their reports Jones based his attack plan. But what the patrols did not see was the row of trenches along Darwin Hill: the contours hid them from view. And it was charging those that 'H' Jones was killed. *Myth No. 5* is that Jones died in an act of suicidal folly. The truth is that A Company were pinned down outside Darwin by fire from the easternmost trenches of that defence line. Jones came up with his small Tactical HQ team to see for himself, and led a two-pronged charge on the trench ahead. It was incredibly brave, but not quite suicidal. What nobody realised, however, was that a chain of six trenches stretched to the west. As Jones' group charged, the next trench in the line opened up with a machine-gun. After that, once A Company realised what they were up against, they used their 66mm anti-tank rockets to obliterate each trench in turn. Twenty minutes after Jones' death, the Argentines round Darwin surrendered. *Myth No. 6*, finally, is that after two of them had been

The first wounded brought back to Ajax Bay hospital (*left*). The helicopter pilots did extraordinary feats that day, actually lifting out wounded from that post directly under the front line. They flew knowing the Argentine observation post would call down mortar fire as soon as they approached. One pilot, Captain John Greenhalgh, even lifted four off the *forward* slope of Darwin Hill, in direct sight of the enemy, at last light. He found them by flying on south until the enemy shot at him. Then he knew where he was. Later, hearing that a Para officer (a friend, in fact) lay dying on the other edge of the battle, where B Company were pinned down, he flew in the dark. He had no night instruments and navigated with a torch to see a map on his knee. He found the man, brought him back and saved his life.

Two Sea Kings even made it on one trip to the casualty station (*right*). All pilots flew at this height all the way down, following the track which is the main road of the isthmus. By now the enemy positions on this part of the line had given up, but from Goose Green the enemy gunners still rained in shells, firing howitzers and anti-aircraft guns horizontally at the Para trenches. The blasts set the gorse alight and a blanket of smoke (*below*) hung over the shambles, as men looked for Argentine wounded and began to bring down the Paras' dead. Some Argentines lay wounded for 48 hours.

The Argentines' view (*left*). It shows the appallingly open ground the Paras had to cross. You are by the enemy bunkers on Darwin Hill. Below is the gorse, with the fold where 'H' Jones died and where the medical post was. Prisoners are being led towards you. Just after dawn next day the Argentines surrendered and (*below*) the Paras began to walk down the long slope into the settlement. The Argentines laid down their weapons and kit (*bottom*) in a ceremony on the grass airstrip. The weapons were gathered up; the helmets remained, an enduring image of defeat.

So many were taken prisoner (983 at the surrender; 20 more later, plus a hundred or so taken during the battle) that they were put into the sheep-shearing shed (*below*) and left to themselves. Much of the enemy ammunition was in a dangerous state. Napalm was leaking (*right*) from its aircraft drop-tanks. More than 200 Argentines were killed. (The Paras lost 17.) Parties of sad prisoners were set to bringing their dead from the battlefield (*below*) and preparing them for mass burial. That Sunday, 2 Para's padre, David Cooper, held an open air Remembrance Service (*far right*). The Para dead were buried on a slope over San Carlos.

shot by an enemy trench showing a White Flag, the Paras took no prisoners. That incident came late in the day, and Lt Jim Barry and his platoon sergeant, of D Company, were killed. Whether it was treachery or muddle, nobody knows. It was true that in the attack which immediately followed, the siege of the schoolhouse north of Goose Green (see the map) by C Company and the survivors of Barry's platoon, no prisoners were taken. But nobody tried to surrender: the ammunition in the schoolhouse exploded, incinerating the defenders inside it. News of the White Flag incident did not reach the rest of the battlefield for some time; by then it was dusk, and 2 Para's log records: 'As darkness fell the fighting quietened. The shelling of mortar fire ceased and the devastating anti-aircraft artillery stopped.' That night, Major Chris Keeble, the second-in-command of 2 Para who had taken over when Jones was killed, wrote his grim ultimatum to the defenders of Goose Green.

THE CHOPPERS' WAR

'They were wonderful. Just when you thought "God, I really need a helicopter now" there it would be, coming over some fold in the ground like the Seventh Cavalry. They were the bravest of anyone. Superb.'

Para doctor

'Oddly enough, it's easy to be calm. The point is that the helicopter engine makes such a noise that you can't hear any gunfire outside. It's quite peaceful, in a way.'

Helicopter pilot

5 Brigade joins the force

Captain Peter Jackson, master of QE2, is convinced: 'She was the only ship in the world that could have done the job. If QE2 hadn't been used, the war would definitely have been longer.' The job was to ferry south 3,300 men, among them the Scots and Welsh Guards and the Gurkhas. They set sail from Southampton on May 12. And QE2 was the 'only ship' because she ran down to South Georgia at 29 knots non-stop, sailing alone because no naval vessel could sustain that speed. (In all, QE2 sailed 16,000 miles in less than a month, a record for a ship of that size.)

As they passed 50 miles west of Ascension, keeping over the horizon so nobody could spot them, helicopters flew out from the island bearing the man going down to take command of the Falklands land forces, Major-General Jeremy Moore, and his 200 staff. Then the great vessel zig-zagged south. 'What worried us most was the chance of a suicide mission by an Argentine submarine,' Jackson says. So the ship sailed without lights – its portholes blacked out – and without its radar. Radar emissions can be detected, so it was switched on again only when QE2 had to weave, in fog, between the icebergs of the South Atlantic. On the evening of May 27, in darkness and dense fog, QE2 sailed into Grytviken harbour, South Georgia. Waiting for her was Canberra.

Canberra's task – while QE2 sailed home with survivors from Ardent, Antelope and Coventry – was to take 5 Brigade into San Carlos Water. Privately, Canberra's naval chief, Captain Christopher 'Beagle' Burne, doubted if The Great White Whale, as the troops called her, would survive a second trip into 'Bomb Alley'. But Canberra did survive, to begin disgorging the 1,200 combat troops at Port San Carlos on May 31.

The initial plan was for these to garrison the beach-head and relieve 2 Para at Goose Green, freeing Marines and Paras for the push on Stanley. But then Major-General Moore announced a change. Now 5 Brigade would go forward, while 40 Commando stayed behind. Military politics were in part behind this, though Moore also worried that the enemy might counter-attack on the beach-head. The CO of 40 Commando, Lt Col. Malcolm Hunt, was of course chagrined. But the flamboyant CO of 5 Brigade, Brigadier Tony Wilson, seized his chance. He co-opted 2 Para from Goose Green; and on June 4 the world learned how Wilson had leapt 36 miles round the southern flank by the ingenious wheeze of phoning the manager of the Fitzroy Settlement, checking no Argentines were there and flying forward in his helicopter. The call was actually made by a major in 2 Para; and Wilson's helicopter was within seconds of being shot down by his own forces. But it was a bold stroke. Wilson had made it to Fitzroy and Bluff Cove. Getting the Guards up, however, was to bring tragedy.

MAY 31

'I've grabbed my land in this great jump forward'

Brigadier Tony Wilson, 5 Brigade CO

The secret rendezvous at South Georgia. As dawn breaks on the mountains above Grytviken harbour, QE2 starts shifting the men and stores of 5 Brigade into Canberra for the final run into 'Bomb Alley', San Carlos Water.

5 Brigade lands. In the
foreground men dig in, having
already scrounged corrugated
iron for roofing. Below them
the containers line along the
prefabricated metal roadway.
In the background troops
march to their dispersal areas,
these late arrivals filing
through the positions already
dug by earlier units. Overhead,
a Sea King totes a truck.

Brigadier Wilson of 5 Brigade
insisted on bringing with him
these massive 0.5 inch
Browning machine-guns
(*opposite*). They devastated
enemy bunkers in the final
battles. As the landing craft
plied on in the dusk (*above*) the
three land commanders met on
the Falklands for the first time
(*left*): left to right, Brigadier
Julian Thompson of 3
Commando Brigade, Wilson,
and Major-General Jeremy
Moore.

'We'll pound them,' said Thompson before the final battles; and for days the British guns, draped in camouflage netting on the lower slopes behind Mount Kent (*right*), shelled enemy positions. (Some bunkers on Longdon had 20 feet of roofing to protect them, though.) Two units of the Royal Artillery went to war: 29 Commando Regiment and 4th Field Regiment. They joined

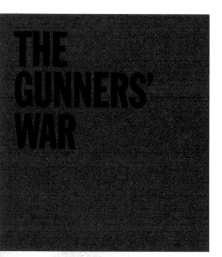

THE GUNNERS' WAR

forces for the final assault. Both fired 105 mm guns, which could be lifted forward by Wessex (*far right*). That was the bottleneck. After Goose Green, Thompson ordered that all guns have double ration of shells: 15,000 rounds in all. To move so many took days. But the effort was justified. By dawn after the last battles some guns were left with only six shells. The Navy also laid down heavy fire from the 4.5 inch guns of Avenger, Glamorgan, Arrow and Yarmouth. The gunners were so accurate they were landing shells 50 yards in front of British troops.

The fire was so fierce because a bomb had gone into Galahad's ammunition hold. By lucky chance, helicopters were already on the scene, ferrying kit up to 5 Brigade HQ, so they were over the ship almost at once.

Tragedy at Bluff Cove

Afterwards, some recalled hearing a 'whoosh'. Their instant thought was that it sounded like one of their own Blowpipe missiles being fired. Then, a second later, came another 'whoosh'. And suddenly it was a nightmare.

'I heard the roar of the jets coming over,' one of the officers on Sir Galahad remembered. 'Just as they piped Action Stations there were two loud explosions. Suddenly there was a flash of flame and the cabin filled with dust. The door flew open. The amazing thing was how much damage was done. The whole place was in a horrible mess, even places a long way from the explosions. There were people everywhere, crawling on their hands and knees below the smoke...'

It was, for Britain, *the* disaster of the war. The bombing of the supply ships Sir Galahad and Sir Tristram left 53 dead and 46 injured, mostly young Welsh Guardsmen. Why did it happen? Different men give different answers. Some date its origins two weeks before, to May 25 when the container ship Atlantic Conveyor had been sunk. The helicopters she carried were to have ferried the troops forward to the mountains above Stanley. Without them, everyone had to walk – or go by ship. Others trace the disaster back to June 1 when Major-General Moore, under political pressure, changed his plans and sent the Guards of 5 Brigade, rather than the Marines of 40 Commando, round the southern flank. Commandos, the argument runs, could have walked. Guards, fresh from London ceremonial duties, could not. Still others point the finger at the War Cabinet. Shaken by the losses in San Carlos Water, Mrs Thatcher and her ministers had decreed that the navy was not to lose another major vessel. But for that order, the navy would have escorted Sir Galahad and Sir Tristram round the coast precisely to protect them from air attack.

The debate remains, though, about whether or not the tragedy was avoidable. Should the Welsh Guards have disembarked more promptly from Sir Galahad? The evidence suggests that, if they had fully appreciated the danger, they might have done so before the raid took place.

The first wave of 5 Brigade, six hundred men of the Scots Guards, sailed round from Port San Carlos late on June 5 aboard Intrepid. But off the south coast Intrepid, fearing the land-based Exocet missiles at Stanley, launched the Guards at dead of night into landing craft some miles out to sea. Swept off course by rip-tides and thrown about by 70 knot winds, the landing craft took seven hours to get into Bluff Cove – with three troopers suffering from exposure. Next night, June 6, Fearless brought the second wave: six hundred men of the Welsh Guards. But now the weather was so bad that less than half could get off. Fearless sailed back in the darkness to San Carlos; and over the next day, June 7, the 350 soldiers still aboard were

A Rapier battery had been in position over the anchorage for some hours; but its electronics had been shaken up bu its journey and, despite frantic efforts by its crew (*above*) to re-take it, the battery was still not in action when the attack came.

transferred into Sir Galahad – which could take the risk of running them directly ashore. That night they set off once more.

But Sir Galahad brought the men not into Bluff Cove, but into the inlet called Port Pleasant, which leads up to Fitzroy. By dawn it was anchored a quarter of a mile offshore, alongside Sir Tristram, which was delivering kit to 5 Brigade HQ on the shore there. Bluff Cove to Fitzroy is four miles by sea. But by land, because a bridge had been blown by the Argentines, the march would have been a circuitous 12 miles. The Guards decided to stay aboard, watching video films.

This is the only picture taken at Bluff Cove of the helicopter pilot's eye view as they neared the stricken ship. As they worked waves of heat rose up to meet them, and small arms ammunition exploding in the blaze whined around them. Any approach to the ship was highly dangerous. But with extraordinary skill and bravery, the pilots flew time after time into that black cloud, and hovered there blind, so their winchmen could pull up the survivors. When some of Galahad's life rafts drifted back towards the burning vessel, the pilots took their helicopters down almost to water level so the wash from their rotor blades would drive the dinghies away again.

The survivors, some horribly
wounded, were flown to 2
Para's aid post on the shore.

Towards lunchtime, a Marine officer brought landing craft out to them. He was worried. An enemy observation post was known to be in the hills; and a Canberra reconnaissance aircraft had flown high overhead the night before. Air raids were still a daily happening: there had been an alert earlier that morning. He urged the Guards to land – land anywhere, but land now. The Guards replied that his landing craft were dangerous: they had ammunition piled aboard. Besides, they wanted to sail to Bluff Cove.

At 5.15 pm, just as the BBC World Service News was finishing – and as the Welsh Guards finally began to disembark – two Skyhawks skimmed low into the inlet from the south-east. Both ships were hit, Sir Tristram the more seriously so all landing craft were diverted to her. Twenty minutes later came a second bombing run: a pair of Mirages. There was a huge explosion aboard Sir Galahad, a pall of smoke and billowing flame. Those on shore watched the horror unfold, helpless.

The disaster effectively
destroyed 1 Welsh Guards as a
fighting unit, for all their kit
was lost too.

An army mirrors its society. The elite among Argentina's forces, its pilots, were brave and superbly trained. The gunners were skilled with the 105 mm howitzers. And the marines were tough professionals. But a gulf between officers and their men sapped the morale of the unskilled conscripts, even though their kit was in fact first class.

THE ARGENTINES' WAR

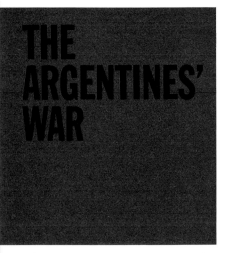

Colour film removed from
Argentine prisoners shows
(*below*) the war they saw.

A captured Argentine officer is
led away blindfold (*below
right*) for interrogation.

'Dear Son, I hope that when these lines reach your hands you will
be in good health and high spirit and with a lot of faith, as we
have, that you will both be home soon. I, son, have much
confidence that our Lord Jesus Christ will protect all our sons,
because at this moment all soldiers are our sons and I think that
we mothers feel the same way about you all and are with you in
spirit all the time. There is no need to worry about me. I am calm
now. At first I was worried for my two sons but now I understand
that by worrying I gain nothing because I know the Lord will
protect you through the night . . .
. . . I will be watching out for both my sons and all the others and
hoping that soon you will be home with me and your father and
brothers who are missing you terribly. Regards and love from
your brother and your father, and I send all my love to you. Love
to your brother and the same to Miguel and Pedro if you see
them'
Letter found on Argentine killed on Mount Harriet

The longest march

The war gave a word to the language. Fittingly, it was the least 'glamorous' phase of the campaign which is thus commemorated. The word is 'yomping', Marine slang for a long march under heavy kit. In Para language it is 'tabbing', which deserves record too because the men of 45 Commando and 3 Para did it together: the long march across the north of the island from Ajax Bay on San Carlos Water eastwards in an arc to Estancia House and on again to the mountains overlooking Stanley for the final battles.

It was an epic march, the longest carrying full kit across rough country in the history of the Commandos. Forty miles, with kit weighing up to 120 lbs. The chronicler of this Herculean effort was the journalist Charles Laurence, who marched with what he called the 'bootneck Marines' of 45 Commando and who afterwards recorded ruefully that 'my boots, issued new on board Canberra just three weeks ago, [when journalists were kitted out], now

MAY 26– JUNE 4

'The only difference between us and Hannibal is that he had elephants and we walked'

Brig. Julian Thompson

One of 45 Commando's mortar platoon sets out on the long march (*left*): he has dumped his kit on a command vehicle.
Above: 45 digging in amid the eerie calm of Teal Inlet.

look as if they have been in service since World War Two.'

'We have yomped,' he wrote, 'ankle-deep in marshland, waded rivers, hauled up mountains. We have kept going through up to six hours of darkness, stumbling through the tussock grass. Sleet, snow and torrential rain have fallen. Where possible we have taken refuge in farm buildings, where the first task has been to dry out boots and sleeping bags to prevent trench foot and assure rest. We have eaten meals – "scran" – cold to avoid the giveaway light of a hexamine cooking stove.'

On May 29 the Paras reached the haven of Teal Inlet, one of the rare spots

The ends of the march: 45's officers pose for a 'school portrait' in the bracken of Ajax Bay; while at Estancia House 3 Para's CO, Lt Col. Hew Pike, stands proudly outside the startling dugout constructed by one of his sergeants, Graham Colbeck. 'Give him 24 hours,' said Pike, 'and you would think Sergeant Colbeck had been on the Somme for three years.'

RSM Pat Chapman (*top*) leads HQ Company of 45 Commando out of Teal Inlet on the last leg of their march to the mountains. The file of men wound for two miles; and, to keep radio silence, messages were passed back man to man down the line. Already at Estancia House, meanwhile, 3 Para at last have time to wash, shave and set up camp.

on the Falklands where trees survive. They rested only briefly before pressing on in a snow-storm to Estancia House and the foothills of the mountains above Stanley. By now the Northern Route had generated such grim life of its own that, back in San Carlos, Brigadier Julian Thompson seriously feared 3 Para might march on Stanley *on their own*, and flew forward personally to stop them. Behind the Paras, following a more winding coastal route, came the slogging files of 45 Commando. 'In 1945,' their CO, Lt Col. Andy Whitehead said, 'the infantry walked from Normandy to Berlin. So we can walk to Stanley.' In the end, they did just that.

ENDURING

'I love them, the grubby little youths. Of course they are horrible: fit for the Hitler Youth, I tell them. But they are marvellous. They'll walk patiently all day and they'll endure anything'

Commando Rifle Coy CO

Filmed by the combat camera of his Harrier, the sequence of pictures (*right*) shows the destruction of two Mirages in a single sortie on May 24 by Lt Comm. Andy Auld, CO of 899 RN Squadron, flying off Hermes. Each triplet of pictures records the firing of one of Auld's Sidewinder missiles and its explosion on target. The combat took place off Pebble Island.

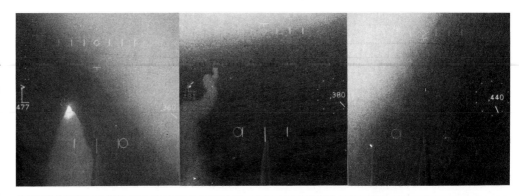

THE HARRIERS' WAR

They laid a short portable runway at Port San Carlos: thousands of metal strips that interlocked to form a wide path up a gentle slope by the water. No ordinary aircraft could have used it but it was a perfect base for the Harriers (*right*). But nobody really got used to seeing a fully-armed Harrier rising (*below*) from the middle of a moor. But it meant the carriers could stay safely to the east during daylight hours.

'I counted them all out and I counted them all back.' This reassurance by BBC-TV reporter Brian Hanrahan was one of the memorable phrases of the campaign. But of course the Harriers did suffer losses during the war: eight were lost, and three of their pilots were killed. But the Harriers accounted for 43 Argentine aircraft and they never lost in air combat. There were simply too few. The daily 'Air Combat Control' was not extensive enough to stave off all enemy air attack, particularly when their pilots began to fly in low from unexpected directions. The Harriers frequently caught those planes on their way home but by then, as at Bluff Cove, the damage had usually been done. Yet the Argentine Air Force paid an appalling price: total losses were probably 110 aircraft, including 70 front-line jets.

Both RAF and Naval Harriers sailed with the Task Force. As they neared the islands, even those on Alert had to be lashed to Hermes' deck (*left*) between flights. The RAF Harrier (*right*: note the radar in its nose is a different shape from the RN version on the left) waited armed up with Sidewinders, though the missile warheads still had their safety caps fitted.

The final battles

'The misty scene as dawn broke will be perhaps the most haunting memory of this long, cold fight. The debris of battle was scattered along the length of the mountain, encountered round every turn in the rocks, in every gully. Weapons, clothing, rations, boots, tents, ammunition, sleeping bags, blood-soaked medical dressings, packs – all abandoned, along with the recoilless rifles, mortars and machine-guns that had given us so much trouble during darkness. The enemy lay dead everywhere . . . Standing amid the shell holes and shambles of battle and watching the determined, triumphant but shocked, saddened faces of those who had lost their friends, the Iron Duke's comment was never more apt: "There is nothing half so melancholy as a battle won, unless it is a battle lost" . . .'

Hew Pike, CO of 3 Para, wrote that about Mount Longdon, one of the five night attacks which settled the war. In its evocation of fatigue and horror

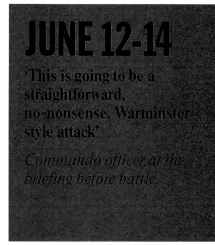

JUNE 12-14

'This is going to be a straightforward, no-nonsense, Warminster style attack'

Commando officer at the briefing before battle

The terrain and its cost: This soldier of 3 Para (*opposite*) has been through the battle for Mount Longdon. The panorama (*left*) was the view from Anchor, 42 Commando's post on Mount Kent. Left to right stretch the twin breasts of Two Sisters, the fin of Goat Ridge, in the distance Tumbledown, then Mount William and, extreme right, Mount Harriet. Below is the rough model constructed by Pike, 3 Para's CO (seen admiring it, right, with Robert Fox, BBC). The white tape is the Start Line for attacks. The road winds back to Stanley. Left of it is Mount Longdon, 3 Para's objective that night. Right of the road lie Two Sisters and Mount Harriet, front, with Tumbledown behind. Viewed together, the pictures show how Longdon, Two Sisters and Mount Harriet made a north-south defence line, which had to be taken simultaneously, because each could fire on to the other. But Tumbledown and Mount William could come in Phase Two.

MOUNT LONGDON

Men of 3 Para instinctively cower as another shell comes in. The wounded man they were tending died as this picture was taken. He was the Argentine, blinded by a bullet through both temples, who earlier stared sightless at the camera (*far right*). The shelling was accurate and intense, and the Paras huddled against the rocks (*right*) for shelter. But there were still casualties (*centre*) which the Scout helicopters flew in to pick up even while the shells fell round them.

after the explosion of violence which climaxed the campaign in the Falklands, it could stand for any of the battles. In essence, British troops fought their way up five steep and rocky hillsides, sown with mines, swept by artillery and mortar and machine-gun fire. 'They kept coming through the mortar fire,' a young Argentine prisoner said afterwards. 'It was incredible. You are the bravest and most professional troops in the world.'

Moore had hoped to launch his offensive on the anniversary of D-Day, June 6. The troops were mostly in place. 42 Commando and the SAS had been shivering for a week in the snow on the westernmost peak, Mount

Left: Moore (right) plans the final battles with Thompson (centre). Their artillery adviser, Colonel Pennicot, looks on. Moore did think initially of an assault on a narrower front, the idea being to keep rolling into Stanley. But he finally decided on the slower, peak by peak attack, in part to give the Argentine general time to foresee his defeat and surrender before there had to be a bloody battle for Stanley, which would have destroyed the town.

MOUNT HARRIET
The final Orders Group by the CO of 42 Commando, Nick Vaux (*left*). 'Unlike in Northern Ireland where normally casualties take precedence over operations, for obvious reasons that cannot be so here...' Vaux had already told his men. After the O Group, many soldiers wrote last letters home (*above*).

Kent. But that weather, and Bluff Cove, held things up, especially the ferrying of ammunition to the gunners already pounding enemy positions from the foot of Mount Kent. It was finally decided that the attack would start at 2 am on Saturday June 12 and run in two phases over two nights.

Phase One: 3 Para would press forward to overrun Mount Longdon, which dominated the northern route. Simultaneously, 42 Commando would advance south-east from Mount Kent and Mount Challenger on to Mount Harriet and, hopefully, Goat Ridge. Then 45 Commando would attack Two Sisters.

Phase Two: Next night, 2 Para would circle north-east behind 3 Para on Mount Longdon and take Wireless Ridge, actually overlooking Stanley. To the south, the Scots Guards and Gurkhas would attack Tumbledown and then press on to Mount William on the outskirts of the town. 'We'll get everything together, pound their positions with gunfire and go in on a night attack,' said an officer giving briefings on the overall battle plan. By first light on Sunday, June 13, it should all be over.

The outcome was rather messier. 3 Para crossed the Start Line 15 minutes late (punctual compared to other units). They were heading for Full Back

MOUNT HARRIET
By dawn, 42 Commando had taken Harriet. This pair on its peak (*above*) were in J-Juliet Company, made up of the Marines who had been forced to surrender to the initial Argentine invaders, been shipped home, and were now fighting their way back to Stanley, carrying a Falkland Islands flag to raise there.

The importance of mortar fire in all the British attacks (*below*) lay in its accuracy and the speed with which it could be zeroed-in on targets by Forward Fire Controllers up at the front line. But hauling up shells was a problem: they are carried in pairs in tubes: a tube-full weighs 26 lbs.

and Fly Half, as they had named the east and west peaks of Longdon. It was to have been a silent advance, but then on Full Back the corporal commanding the most forward section of B Company stepped on a mine 600 yards short of the Argentine positions and the enemy opened fire. The Argentine troops could see at night: they had hundreds of pairs of 'passive night goggles', which are infra-red spectacles. The British had nothing as good. To clear the enemy positions, 3 Para were calling in artillery and 300 salvoes of naval gunfire (from Avenger) on targets only 50 yards ahead of them – 'superb precision,' Pike said of the gunnery. It took 3 Para six hours to clear

Fly Half and another four hours to capture Full Back. They finished the job with bayonets: 'Many still had their bayonets fixed as they grimly cleared back through the position in the thick dawn mist', Pike recalled. 3 Para lost 22 killed, 47 wounded. There were more than 50 enemy dead, 39 prisoners, ten wounded.

On Mount Harriet, meanwhile, 42 Commando achieved more surprise. 42's CO, Nick Vaux, had codenamed the peak Zoya after his elder daughter; Goat Ridge he called Tara after the younger. The Argentines had, logically, expected an attack from the west, but 42 crept along the road running south

MOUNT HARRIET
The battle ended at dawn, but with hundreds of enemy soldiers still hidden on the mountain, many afraid they would be shot if they surrendered. A corporal of L Company sent out a Marine to look for a missing pair of men; they came back with 40 prisoners. Then Argentines began trudging down in numbers that astounded 42 Commando. They gathered on the road from which the attack had started. There the wounded were given water and first aid (*above*). *Left:* 42 moving off to a new position.

TUMBLEDOWN

The Scots Guards were flown
forward from Bluff Cove the
afternoon before the battle (*top
left*). They at once began to dig
in (*top right*). You are there
looking south-east. The
shadow of Goat Ridge falls
across from the left. Around
1.00 am they began to advance
in company waves over the
saddle to the left and down
into the open ground in front
of Tumbledown. Sporadically
through the afternoon the
enemy shelled them as they
dug in. One shell in this
barrage (*centre*) has hit a
phosphorus grenade carried on
a Guardsman's webbing that
he has taken off to dig his
trench. Caught in the middle of
the bursts is a Scorpion light
tank of the Blues & Royals.
Around dusk they all tried to
eat. Their padre, Major Angus
Smith (*above*), was seen to
have a hearty appetite.

of the hill and then came up its south-east face. The enemy swept the attack route with 0.5 inch Browning machine-guns dug into rock bunkers. Vaux decided to use Milan wire-guided missiles, firing up the slope to blast each bunker in turn. 'Pretty expensive,' he said later – a Milan costs £20,000 plus – 'but our job was to get rid of them.' (The Paras had similarly used Milan at Goose Green.) Any Brownings still intact were then turned uphill on the enemy. 42 Commando lost, by some miracle, only one man killed.

With pardonable professional gusto, a young 2nd Lieutenant of 45 Commando reflected later on the 'unique experience' afforded by Two Sisters: 'a

TUMBLEDOWN
At dawn, as prisoners were led back (*left*), everyone was thinking grimly of the next attack: a daylight march on Sapper Hill, on the outskirts of Stanley. Then came news of the Argentine surrender. This group (*below*) – men of 7 Platoon, G Company of 2 Scots Guards – have heard it two minutes before.

full Commando assault on a conventional army in a well prepared defensive position'. He remembered the moment that firing started: 'A nervous sentry, obviously panicking having seen our advance troops, threw a hand illuminant into the darkness. This was ideal for our purposes, because not only did it warn us, but it also confirmed the location of two important fire trenches ... As the cliché goes, all hell let loose.' Two Sisters cost 45 Commando four dead and 11 wounded.

Phase Two was just as tough, particularly because it was delayed 24 hours, so the units had to endure another day's uncomfortably accurate Argentine shelling. In 2 Para's assault on Wireless Ridge, it is the courage of the mortar platoon which is remembered. If mortar fire is to be pinpoint accurate, the mortar's base-plate has to be securely anchored. But at a crucial moment in the attack, one base-plate began to slip on the rocky slope. One after another, four soldiers stood on the plate as the vital rounds were fired – knowing as they did that, one after another, their ankles would be broken by the recoil shock of each round.

The Scots Guards' assault on Tumbledown was a classic night action.

Giving final orders, their CO, Mike Scott, said to his officers: 'Tell your men that if we start getting shelled or mortared, they have got to keep walking through it and ignore it if anyone goes down. Because if they lie down they will not stand up again. They will be too frightened.' The Guards did not lie down. The Argentine flares hung in the air, and in their stark light shell after shell lobbed among the Guards as they walked steadily forward to the lower slopes and on up the steep sides. Then they used bayonets. By dawn Tumble-down was theirs – but at a cost of nine dead and 41 wounded. It was the last battle of the war.

Marching into Stanley

It was for those who saw it the enduring image of the war. It came an hour or so after dawn on Monday, June 14. Tumbledown had just fallen. 2 Para were on Wireless Ridge, which gave them a fine view. 'Suddenly we saw all these specks running off Sapper Hill,' a Para officer remembered. 'Then we saw them coming off Longdon. All running, running back to Stanley.'

About half an hour later, the Gurkhas' second-in-command, Major Bill Dawson, emerged from the radio of the Gurkhas' reserve HQ on Two Sisters. 'Gentlemen,' he said, 'a white flag has been seen flying over Port Stanley.' There was a moment's silence and then a bursting cheer. It was ten weeks to the day since the first ships of the Task Force had sailed from Portsmouth. (Aboard Fearless, one of those ships, Captain Jeremy Larken gave the news over the Tannoy. 'It looks,' he drawled, 'as though the Arg has folded.')

'Through history,' Major-General Moore mused later, 'there comes a point where there is a collapse of will and suddenly it spreads. It's astonishing the speed with which it spreads, isn't it? A fascinating morning that was.' (So swift was the collapse that Moore had personally to radio HALT messages to Harriers already flying in for a precision strike on Sapper Hill. He stopped them three minutes off target.)

For the troops the main concern now was to get into Stanley as fast as possible, for the severely practical purpose of grabbing the best beds and baths. 2 Para 'legged it' to the racecourse on the edge of Stanley before

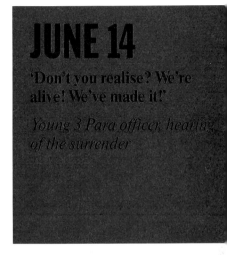

JUNE 14

'Don't you realise? We're alive! We've made it!'

Young 3 Para officer, hearing of the surrender

The advance into Stanley was in some ways the most trying march of the war, because the enemy had laid minefields throughout the area, scattering among the tussock grass saucer-sized anti-personnel mines that would blow a foot off. The nightmare of every soldier was to lose a limb *after* the war was over. So the men of 45 Commando (*opposite*) make a jaunty sight as they march down from Two Sisters, but on either side of that track is a minefield and, though they look casual, each man is in fact walking in the footsteps of another. In the traditional soldiers' symbol of peace, they have taken off their helmets and put on their berets, as 2 Para are doing (*left*) on Wireless Ridge just as they hear news of the white flags.

Brigadier Thompson halted them. 'Exploiting forward, sir,' they said.

The first British soldier into Stanley was actually Captain Rod Bell, the Spanish-speaking Marine. He flew in as Moore's emissary an hour after the white flags. As Bell scrambled through a hedge, the Argentine naval commander, Melbourne Hussey, greeted him: 'We saw you landing in the wrong place.' 'I don't know Stanley quite as well as you do,' Bell replied curtly. For a week, Bell had been beaming secret messages into the town, urging surrender. That morning a Stanley GP, Dr Alison Bleaney, appalled at the prospect of fighting there, had persuaded Hussey to come to the radio in her surgery and, with some moral courage, to respond to Bell's appeal. That was why the white flags had gone up and why Bell now flew in. About 8.00 pm Moore followed, flying through a snowstorm; and at 9.00 pm Falklands time the Argentine commander, General Mario Menendez, signed the surrender document Major-General Moore had brought with him. Then, at last, British troops could start marching into Stanley.

A short way further along their march recorded on the previous page, 45 Commando walked into a minefield. By now snow was falling (*above*) but for 20 minutes each man stood quite still while the Sappers searched for paths through it. Meanwhile for Moore (*top right*) surrender brought a tour shoulder-high round town, meeting babies and sipping assorted drinks. But perhaps the greatest sense of triumph was that felt by men of Landing Party 8901, the Marines who had fought the invasion, as they marched once again into Stanley (*right*).

For the Gurkhas, the first victory was to go at all. The Foreign Office, seeing trouble with Nepal, tried to stop them. In the war, they proved yet again their high reconnaissance skills, rounding up enemy patrols. Their reputation so scared the Argentines that, to the Gurkhas' regret, they fled from Mount William rather than face a Gurkha attack.

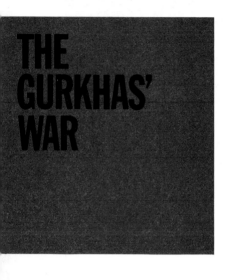

THE GURKHAS' WAR

Seen off on QE2 with the prayers of their *bahun* (*below*), the Gurkhas were remembered on the voyage for their dawn runs (*above right*) and (*below right*) their homesickness at the sight of South Georgia's snowy mountain peaks.

Flying Gurkha style: two inside a Scout, two more on its landing skids, as a patrol sets out to look for a suspected Argentine observation post.

Defence stations at Goose Green (*above*), then into the final battle. Gurkha mortar troops (*right*) after a night of heavy artillery fire on Goat Ridge.

'Usually round this time we have dances and parties, but this year there has been nothing,' one teenaged girl lamented to a journalist arriving on a light tank. A small boy (*right*) is more easily satisfied, aboard a Samson engineering vehicle. Note the KEEP RIGHT sign, legacy of the Argentines' efforts to reorganise the islanders' way of life.

Clearing up the mess

Like the honourable Christian he is, Jeremy Moore went first to console the grieving. He visited John Fowler, the islands' education chief, in whose house the only three civilians to die in the whole affair had been killed – sadly, by British naval gunfire. Moore apologised as best he could: the gunners had been trying to knock out Argentine artillery, and they had thought nobody was living in the houses nearby. Then he went to Stanley Cathedral to thank God for those who had survived. The soldiers who marched to the Service of Thanksgiving that first Sunday of peace, kit gleaming, arms swinging, bore little superficial resemblance to the bone-tired warriors who had trudged into town only days before. But all had friends to mourn, and many at the service sang with tears streaming down their faces. All over the Falklands, indeed, there were quiet obsequies. By their shoreline, on a hill which overlooks both settlements, the people of Goose Green and Darwin built a stone cairn to commemorate 'H' and all his Paras who had died on those peaceful green slopes. On Tumbledown, the Scots Guards put up a tall cross with the names of their dead on it; and their regimental piper stood at the windswept summit playing a new lament, 'The Crags of Tumbledown'.

As Sappers restored essential services, and the Argentine troops began to depart and then the British to follow them, the Falklanders could start to consider their future. The most lethal uncertainty confronting them was the Argentine mines, strewn over the islands and, being plastic, immune to normal detectors. 'I'll never be able to let my children play on the beach again,' one mother wailed. That was an exaggeration; but certainly it will

JUNE 14-26

'The Falkland Islands are once more under the Government desired by their inhabitants. God Save the Queen.'

Maj. Gen. Jeremy Moore

'Now thank we all our God' they sang in Stanley Cathedral at the Thanksgiving Service. And Major-General Moore and one of his aides, Lt Col. Paul Stevenson, sang more lustily than most, because Moore knew better than anyone how much the British victory owed to what Moore himself had called 'miracles' of good luck. Others found more off-beat ways of celebrating: like this young 2 Para officer (*left*) indulging his Scots gallows-humour on Stanley airfield.

take years to clear the 'camp'. Other uncertainties were less tangible but no less taxing. 'They fought for the islands,' Moore said of the Argentines. 'We fought for the islanders.' For the islanders, even so, things could never be the same.

The living called for action too. Moore dispatched Lt Col. Malcolm Hunt to accept the surrender of the Argentine forces on West Falkland. It was a consolation prize for 40 Commando's stint guarding the San Carlos beachhead. Then, looking drained – a different man from the chipper figure who had joined the Task Force at Ascension – Moore gave a press conference to pay his military debts. He praised the navy's fighting quality: 'a tradition that goes back to Drake and Nelson'. He praised the 'superb toughness' of the Marines and Paras; and he had a special word for his youthful soldiers: 'Let anyone complain about the youth of our country at home – by golly, they should have seen them here.' Then he set about clearing 'the clutter of war'.

Bluntly, that meant the Argentines. To general consternation, there turned out to be 11,000 of them in Stanley. The British had expected to find only 6,200. What they had all been doing was hard to fathom – certainly not fighting. Since the British had no immediate way of coping with so vast a number, the Argentines became, in military parlance, 'self-administering'.

For the first couple of days, in fact, victor and vanquished lived together in Stanley in strange harmony. While the British walked, the Argentines still drove. They still had their weapons. Their senior officers still hogged the rooms at the Upland Goose Hotel and colonised its dining room at meals. The evening after the surrender there was a virtual reunion of British and Argentine officers at the Upland Goose. Copious rounds were bought, and home telephone numbers around Buenos Aires and the Home Counties

As the prisoners were moved out to the airfield, they passed through checks at which first their weapons were taken (*above*) and then their kit was searched. The rule was that they could keep as many personal belongings as they liked, so long as they carried them. As the pile of confiscated rifles grew (*left*), several were seen to have Madonnas taped to their butts. The cards came in the Argentine ration packs, along with miniature bottles of whisky and a slip saying they had been packed by patriotic volunteers. The British troops, fed up with their own ration packs, were very envious.

exchanged. It was a weird scene, a fitting close to a weird war.

Rapidly, though, the relationship took a more traditional turn. The Argentines were disarmed and dispossessed of their vehicles and their rooms. General Menendez and his senior staff were taken off to Fearless, to be held until Argentina formally acknowledged defeat. Menendez wept when he was told he could not stay with his men – though at the same moment, it should be said, his officers still in Stanley were being allowed, after much pleading, to keep their pistols as protection against their own troops. After 200 of these rioted one night and burnt down a food store, for no apparent reason,

The first British Hercules lands on the undamaged Stanley runway. (The last Argentine night-flight landed there only hours before the surrender.) The prisoners, meanwhile, were brought into Stanley in groups, set to work for a day clearing up their mess and then moved to the jetty to be shipped out each evening.

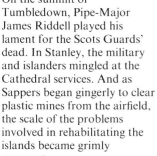

On the summit of Tumbledown, Pipe-Major James Riddell played his lament for the Scots Guards' dead. In Stanley, the military and islanders mingled at the Cathedral services. And as Sappers began gingerly to clear plastic mines from the airfield, the scale of the problems involved in rehabilitating the islands became grimly apparent.

the lot were marched out to the airfield. It was a bleak and bitter place, and a shanty town sprang up as the Argentines hastily converted whatever they could find into rudimentary shelters. Some even lived in the cockpits of wrecked aircraft. Not that British soldiers were faring much better. Some camped in the bombed-out barracks, others endured the local abattoir.

The 500 or so residents of Stanley who had departed for the duration to the 'camp', the interior of the islands, began filtering back. By and large, their neat clapboard homes had been undisturbed by the Argentines; and, by and large, they too had survived the ordeal unscathed. In truth, the Argentines had largely ignored them, just as they now largely ignored the British. (To the chagrin of the troops, both pubs – the Upland Goose and the Globe Tavern – banned soldiers, to conserve supplies.)

In London, meanwhile, there was the dawning realisation that, having regained the islands at such price, Britain now faced the task of garrisoning them against further attack and, presumably, developing them. The cost of either would be millions – cash which Britain had declined to spend on the islands before the invasion.

THE REPORTERS' WAR

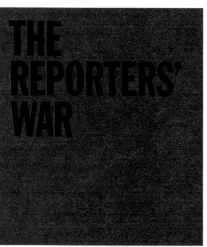

The Ministry of Defence's
'Regulations for
Correspondents' says
shrewdly: 'The essence of
success in war is secrecy; the
essence of success in
journalism is publicity.' From
that clash (and muddle
between London and the
Falklands over what should be
secret) stemmed most of the
arguments about censorship.
But at least the Press saw
everything. Paul Haley (*above*)
of *Soldier Magazine*,
photographed key events. *The
Sun*'s Tony Snow and *Daily
Telegraph*'s A.J. McIlroy were
in the attack on Tumbledown
and (*right*) returned at dawn.

Poor satellite links meant TV film came back by ship. 'Our photo-transmission speed is 20 knots,' said a Defence spokesman. That frustrated both TV crews: (*left*) BBC's Brian Hanrahan, cameraman Bernard Hesketh, soundman John Jockels and, flash-masked, Defence press officer Alan George. But did Whitehall want swift TV pictures of the war?

London *Standard* reporter Max Hastings (*left*) won the Press race into Stanley. Hands over head, he walked in to interview locals at the Upland Goose Hotel. 'Like liberating a suburban golf club,' he said. Many of the Press pictures released in the war were in fact taken by Naval Marine photographer PO Peter Holdgate (*below*), who flew from unit to unit.

'You're the most unmilitary person I've ever met,' one Para told BBC's Robert Fox. 'My 8-year-old daughter could do better than that.' To the amusement of the troops, 28 Pressmen tried to 'hack it': do their job and simultaneously survive. Three quit before the end, three more caught exposure. All saw different phases: IRN's Kim Sabido (*below left*) went forward with 42's Lt Tony Miklinski. Charles Laurence, *Sunday Telegraph*, and Ian Bruce, *Glasgow Herald* (*below right*) yomped with 45. Before the final battles, reporters (*left*) camped on freezing Mount Kent: (from left) Derek Hudson, *Yorkshire Post*; Bruce; Laurence; Robert McGowan, *Daily Express*; John Shirley, *Sunday Times*; Alasdair McQueen, *Daily Mirror*. But what should the Press report? Morale-boosting stories only; or the truth, which inevitably included muddles, rows and tragedy? Most reporters came to identify with the soldiers, in large part because they lived (and could have died) with them.

The rapturous return

The voyage home was eerie. There were fireworks: in mid-Atlantic, as Canberra said farewell to its companion, the supply ship Elk, they fired machine-gun tracer, flares and Bofors shells into the blue equatorial sky. There were high-jinks: a traditional 'sod's opera' of variety turns, with the beefiest sergeants dressed like Danny La Rue. Where they acquired the finery remained a discreet secret. ('Suspenders?' said one baffled colonel. 'On Fearless?') But the celebrations did not keep grief at bay. More than 250 British servicemen had died (and perhaps 1,000 Argentines), and the survivors felt guilt at their good fortune as well as sorrow at their loss. After a fancy dress contest, a Marine corporal began to cry: 'Why did they die? Why did they die?' A young doctor who had worked without pause tortured himself with the fear that he might have saved more men.

Among the letters Major-General Moore had on the Falklands was one from his 11-year-old son, Andrew. 'I hope we are going to win, Daddy,' he wrote. 'I think we will, but I am not shore.' His father had not been sure either. 'Nobody goes to war without doubts,' he said crisply, 'unless he's thick.' But his troops had won – even if Moore knew that it had been, in the words of his favourite general, 'a damned close-run thing.' By the end of the campaign, 90 per cent of his troops had trench-foot, and dysentery was epidemic. At one point there were only two days' food left; and after Goose Green only three days' medical supplies. And it had been a mild Falklands winter. Still, they had won – sloggingly, heroically, against the odds. They sailed up Southampton Water to the reward of an incandescent welcome.

JUNE 26- JULY 11

'You seem to have a few people waiting for you'

Prince Charles, on Canberra in Southampton Water

Canberra going in to berth at Southampton. The Marine captain who took this shot was particularly proud of his timing. 'I held my fire,' he said, 'until the balloons were deployed.' In Buenos Aires, by sad contrast, the junta had clearly decided to risk no public demonstrations. The Argentine troops sailed into Puerto Madryn, an obscure port in Patagonia where, oddly, large numbers of locals speak Welsh. The generals were probably being over-cautious. Where the people of Argentina could greet their returning men (*below left*) they too gave them a rapturous welcome as returning heroes.

Brigadier Julian Thompson, in a stirring end-of-battle message to the men of his 3 Commando Brigade, quoted some lines from Marlowe's 'Tamburlaine':
'I'll have you learn to sleep upon the ground,
March in your armour through watery fens,
Sustain the scorching heat and freezing cold,
Hunger and thirst, right adjuncts of the war,
And after that to scale a city wall,
Beseige a fort to undermine a town,
And make whole cities caper in the air.'
Indeed, that was how the war had been won. As to how it should be celebrated, Major-General Jeremy Moore recalled, as he often did, a comment of the Duke of Wellington: 'Do not congratulate me, Madam. I have lost some of my dearest friends.'

165 days after she left Portsmouth at the head of the Task Force on April 5, the 16,000-ton aircraft carrier HMS Invincible returns to Portsmouth and a tumultuous welcome for her 1,000 crew. (*Photo:* Camera Press/Bryn Cotton)

Chronology

The account in this book has, inevitably, simplified the military complexities – the sheer human effort – of the conflict. So here, extracted from the Ministry of Defence's own matter-of-fact record of events, is the official diary of the campaign on the Falklands.

April 2: Argentine invasion of the Falklands.

April 3: South Georgia taken.

April 5: First Task Force ships, among them Hermes, Invincible and Fearless, sail from Portsmouth. Lord Carrington resigns as Foreign Secretary.

April 7: Britain declares 200 miles 'exclusion zone' around the Falklands.

April 8: US Secretary of State Alexander Haig arrives in London to begin 'shuttle'.

April 9: Canberra sails from Southampton.

April 25: South Georgia retaken.

April 30: US sides with Britain.

May 1: Vulcans and Harriers bomb Stanley airfield.

May 2: Argentine cruiser General Belgrano torpedoed.

May 4: Sheffield hit by Exocet.

May 15: Raid on Pebble Island to knock out enemy airfield and aircraft.

May 21: 3 Cdo Brigade lands on East Falkland. 2 Para and 40 Cdo on Blue Beach. 45 Cdo on Red Beach. 3 Para and 42 Cdo on Green Beach. (Blue Beach is San Carlos Settlement, Red is Ajax Bay and Green Beach is Port San Carlos Settlement.)

May 21/26: consolidation of bridgehead, patrols move forward. Argentine air attacks hit 11 ships.

May 27: 45 Cdo move from Red Beach to Green Beach to start overland move to Douglas Settlement. 3 Para leave Green Beach for Teal Inlet and Estancia. 2 Para move toward Darwin and Goose Green, reach Camilla Creek House by last light.

May 28: Battle of Darwin/ Goose Green. 2 Para attack along isthmus from Burntside House and after bitter fighting were investing Goose Green before dawn May 29. 2 Para lose 17 dead including their CO. J Coy 42 Cdo held at Camilla Creek House to reinforce 2 Para.

May 29: Argentine forces at Goose Green surrender. Over 1,000 prisoners taken. 3 Para reach Estancia House and move to Mount Estancia and Mount Vernet.

May 30: K Coy 42 Cdo seize Mount Kent. Recce group of 5 Infantry Brigade arrive San Carlos.

June 1: 2 Para come under the command of 5 Brigade. 42 Cdo move another company on to Mount Kent.

June 2: Canberra and Norland carrying bulk of 5 Brigade arrive San Carlos Water. Brigade lands on Blue Beach. 1/7 Gurkha Rifles move to Sussex Mountains. 2 Scots Guards move to Verde Mountains and 1 Welsh Guards move to Bonners Bay. 2 Para move forward by helicopter to Fitzroy Settlement and Bluff Cove. A Coy of 1/7 Gurkha Rifles move forward to Goose Green to cover area as 2 Para leave.

June 3: 2 Para complete in Bluff Cove/Fitzroy positions. 29 Battery Royal Artillery in support of 2 Para at Bluff Cove. 3 and 4 Troops of B Squadron Blues & Royals also at Bluff Cove. 42 Cdo completes move to Mount Kent. 79 Royal Artillery join 3 Para at Estancia.

June 4: 1/7 Gurkha Rifles complete move to Goose Green to replace 2 Para and help with evacuation of prisoners.

June 5: 42 Cdo start move onto Mount Challenger. 2 Scots Guards embark at San Carlos for sea journey to Bluff Cove.

June 6: 45 Cdo move on to Mount Kent to relieve 42 Cdo who move to Mount Challenger. 2 Scots Guards arrive Bluff Cove. 1 Welsh Guards embark at San Carlos for move by sea to Bluff Cove. Argentine dead from Darwin/ Goose Green buried at Darwin.

June 7: 1 Welsh Guards Bttln HQ, 1 Rifle Coy and some of Support Coy, at Bluff Cove. The remainder of the battalion returning to San Carlos. Sir Tristram anchored in Port Pleasant and unloaded.

June 8: 1 Welsh Guards' remaining Coy arrive in Port Pleasant on Sir Galahad together with Rapier battery and 16 Field Ambulance. Argentine air attack on Sir Galahad and Sir Tristram and 2 Scots Guards positions at Bluff Cove. 53 dead, 46 injured. Landing craft sunk in Choiseul Sound by Argentine air attack.

June 9: 1/7 Gurkha Rifles, less one company, complete in Bluff Cove, making 5 Brigade complete in that area. Two companies of 40 Cdo put under command of 1 Welsh Guards.

June 10: 2 Para and 1 Welsh Guards under command of 3 Brigade for their attack on Mount Longdon, Two Sisters and Mount Harriet.

June 11/12: 3 Cdo Brigade attack on three axes. 3 Para attack Mount Longdon with 2 Para in reserve. 45 Cdo attack from Mount Kent on to Two Sisters. 1 Welsh Guards secure start line for 42 Cdo who attack from Mount Challenger on to Mount Harriet and Goat Ridge. All positions taken by first light after heavy hand-to-hand fighting.

June 12: 1 Welsh Guards return under command of 5 Brigade.

June 13/14: 5 Brigade Tac HQ established on Goat Ridge. 2 Scots Guards make diversionary attack with troops of Blues & Royals from Mount Harriet towards Mount William. Under cover of this, 2 Scots Guards attack and take Tumbledown Mountain. 1/7 Gurkha Rifles move through 2 Scots Guards' position to assault Mount William. Defenders break and run at dawn, having put up stiff resistance through the night. 1 Welsh Guards make attack to Sapper Hill. White flag flown over Stanley.

June 15: Formal surrender by General Menendez to Major-General Jeremy Moore of all Argentine forces on East and West Falklands. 40 Cdo move to West Falkland to effect surrender there.